Shielded by God's Power

Shielded by God's Power

The Survival Kit: Surviving Childhood Abuse

Volume 1

Ivy Christian

Library of Congress Control Number: 2017910486
ISBN: Hardcover   978-1-5434-3393-7
                 Softcover   978-1-5434-3394-4
                 eBook   978-1-5434-3395-1

Rev. date: 07/03/2017

To order additional copies of this book, contact:
Xlibris
1-888-795-4274
www.Xlibris.com
Orders@Xlibris.com
761288

Foreword

Throughout the Bible, there are inspiring stories of men and women who have overcome great obstacles that have been placed in their lives through their faith and dependence on God. This is just such a story.

It has been my privilege to get to know Ivy both through this story of her life and through our friendship. To know her now, one will never suspect that she has lived anything but an ordinary life. She is a Christian who shares the love of the Lord wherever she goes. She is a caring and giving person, always reaching out to others with her hospitality and generous spirit.

God, through his infinite wisdom, has protected the spirit of his child as he has brought her through a tumultuous childhood. She has endured hardships that will cause some to become bitter. I see no bitterness in her, only a desire to share the love she has for the Lord and a willingness to help others in their times of need.

Ivy has truly forgiven those who have caused her harm. I have learned a lot from her and have tried to apply some of her wisdom in my own life.

This book has been written by Ivy because of her desire to help other people who might have gone through or who are now living through painful and seemingly unendurable things. If she can live through trials and hardships that have been brought about by circumstances completely out of her control, so can you.

It is Ivy's desire that God be given all the glory for maintaining and sustaining her all throughout her life. One of the ways God has sustained her is through other people. She not only has relied on the Lord after she has become a Christian but she is also always involved with people.

To paraphrase Jeremiah 29:11, I believe that the Lord has plans to prosper her, not to harm her, plans to give her a hope and a future. That is our hope as you read her life story.

Sisters Sarah Elmore and Sue Erps
October 10, 2010

Introduction

I began writing about my childhood as a young mother and continued through midlife as my life came apart at the seams stitch by stitch. From third grade, Jesus gave me inner peace through women in the church and through words in songs, which gave me the strength to live above the atrocious and mystifying happenings throughout my childhood.

He, the perfect God, never sinned; however, he suffered rejection and horrible abuse on planet Earth to the ultimate degree from us, his own creation. How could I escape if I was truly his child? Jesus, and only Jesus, knew how to comfort frail humans at all ages through evils and tribulations, such as I experienced at the whim of others. I have never felt satisfied or accepted on planet Earth from three years of age.

However, this was not my permanent home. I became heavenward bound not until the age of forty not because I was better than anyone else but because God loved me enough to send his perfect Son, Jesus, from heaven to become the sacrificial Lamb that shed his blood on the cross of Calvary for my sin nature and all humanity. I had just turned eight years old when, for the first time, I heard of God and his Son, Jesus Christ. Patsy, my playmate at school, introduced me to Sunday school at the Kee Street Methodist Church. I did whatever was necessary to be in church every time the doors opened. No one used harsh words with me, or I would have stopped going to church. I desperately needed to overcome the ugly, fat, and dirty feeling I had developed since becoming a secretly abused child in the last five years.

Once introduced to church, I took comfort in the words to the songs "Jesus Loves Me" and "What a Friend We Have in Jesus" while being whipped. Unknown to me at the time, this was the ingredient to mentally survive the abusive life. Nevertheless, I had to struggle thirty-two more years in church before I came to an intimate relationship with the Shepherd. God protected my mind until I could comprehend that I was not a Christian just because Jesus was real to me as an abused child. By the time I became a Christian, I had learned the phrase "Love is stronger than hate."

What we know about a person is only the tip of an iceberg. That is one of my reasons for writing an autobiography—to help us not to judge others because we can never know all the events, feelings, and emotions of anyone.

> Do not judge, or you too will be judged. For in the same way you judge others, you will be judged, and with the measure you use, it will be measured to you. Why do you look at the speck of sawdust in your brother's eye and pay no attention to the plank in your own eye? How can you say to your brother, "Let me take the speck out of your eye," when all the time there is a plank in your own eye? You hypocrite, first take the plank out of your own eye, and then you will see clearly to remove the speck from your brother's eye. (Jesus Christ)

We can never know what a child is thinking at any given situation. They might forget thoughts as they grow older, but some feelings, which have been embedded in their souls, can motivate bad reactions for the rest of their life.

"Train a child in the way he should go, and when he is old he will not turn from it" (King Solomon).

"I tell you the truth, unless you change and become like little children you will never enter the kingdom of heaven. Therefore, whoever humbles himself like this child is the greatest in the kingdom of heaven. And whoever welcomes a little child like this in my name welcomes me. But if anyone causes one of these little ones who believe in me to sin, it would be better for him to have a large millstone hung around his neck and to be drowned in the depths of the sea" (Jesus Christ).

As you would read in this book, I was beaten and misjudged by my siblings most of my childhood, and Jesus Christ had to take me through many trials to learn to love and forgive my enemies.

> You have heard that it was said, "Love your neighbor and hate your enemy." But I tell you: Love your enemies and pray for those who persecute you, that you may be sons of your Father in heaven. He causes his sun to rise on the evil and the good, and sends rain on the righteous and the unrighteous. If you love those who love you, what reward will you get? Are not even the tax collectors doing that? And if you greet only your brothers, what are you doing more than others? Do not even pagans do that? Be perfect, therefore, as your heavenly Father is perfect. (Jesus Christ)

Another big reason for revealing my past is too many people, like myself, have stuffed their real self deep down inside until they play games of being someone they are not. This is the century of having no wrinkles on our faces, eyebrows curved just the perfect way, and foundation applied as if we have been air-sprayed. What is wrong with aging? What is wrong with society accepting who we are and where we've been as we progress through life? It is time in this still free society when all things are accepted that the ones who have lived horrendous existences be freed.

Ivy Christian
October 10, 2010

One day the angels came to present themselves before the Lord, and Satan also came with them. The Lord said to Satan, "Where have you come from?"

Satan answered the Lord, "From roaming through the earth and going back and forth in it."

Then the Lord said to Satan, "Have you considered my servant Job? There is no one on earth like him; he is blameless and upright, a man who fears God and shuns evil."

"Does Job fear God for nothing?" Satan replied. "Have you not put a hedge around him and his household and everything he has? You have blessed the work of his hands, so that his flocks and herds are spread throughout the land. But stretch out your hand and strike everything he has, and he will surely curse you to your face."

The Lord said to Satan, "Very well, then, everything he has is in your hands, but on the man himself do not lay a finger."

—Job 1:9–12

M y name was Ivy. I was a carefree two-and-a-half-year-old living with my teenage mother and my granddaddy Ooking in a three-room apartment in an upstairs town house in Baltimore, Maryland.

One afternoon, I followed my teenage mother into the living room to answer the door; and her sister, her husband, and their little girl, Marsha, entered the apartment. I followed Mother back to the kitchen, begging, "Mommy, Mommy, please let Marsha and me eat at my table."

"Ivy, do you and your cousin promise to eat dinner and not play?"

Together, we danced up and down, shouting, "Yes, yes, we promise!"

My cousin and I sat on the child-size chairs in the corner of the small kitchen while the adults sat on their big chairs. We both were proud of our feet touching the floor just like Mommy, Granddad Ooking, my aunt, and my uncle. Soon the excitement of having company at my table wore off, and I asked my cousin, "Would you like to go downstairs and play a trick on the neighbors?"

She stood up with a big smile on her face and excitedly replied, "Yes." I placed my finger over my lips to indicate that we had to be quiet as we tiptoed out of the kitchen while all four of the adults were talking at once.

We ran down the steep steps to the front porch. Marsha followed my lead and tiptoed onto the large front porch of the town house next door. I rang the doorbell, and she ran behind me as fast as our little legs would carry us to scrunch down beside the concrete steps. We actually believed that no one could see us or hear our giggling. When the neighbor came to the door and found no one there, we ran to the next porch, laughing.

By the time we got to the end of the block, I felt comfortable going up on the porch of my favorite neighbor and ringing the doorbell as I had many times before. Only this time, she came out of her house; and in a gentle tone, she let me know that I had not been fooling anyone except myself. "I know you are hiding by the steps, and stop ringing my doorbell."

Immediately, my face felt red-hot, and my stomach hurt. I managed to jump up, and I outran my cousin back to our apartment. We tiptoed up the steps and passed the adults still debating on an issue. Happily, I sat down on my little chair, where I felt secure in my little world in our little kitchen.

I loved the activity in the kitchen where Mother fastened laundry to a line, which reeled from the kitchen window out to a pole across the alley. She made me laugh as she pulled the line, sending the clothes out, high over the back alley, where most often children were playing ball below.

Also from that window, sometimes I would see a donkey-driven vegetable cart passing through the alley with a man singing, "Tomatoes, potatoes, cucumbers, watermelons." My mother and I would run with the other women in the neighborhood to inspect the ripe red tomatoes and watermelons. I found joy and happiness in a world where I believed that I was the center of the universe.

In 1938, Granddad Ooking left his building supply business in the care of his only son, Ben, and rented an apartment hundreds of miles away from Baltimore because his beautiful homecoming-queen teenage daughter had become pregnant by her teenage fiancé.

Granddad Ooking wanted to protect his popular daughter, Martha, and me from the small-town gossip in the Appalachian Mountains.

Either my teenage mother or Granddad Ooking read to me or took me for walks. Most often, Mother sent us to the upper end of the block for items from the neighborhood market. My favorite trip took us to the lower end of the block. As we walked past the neighbors sitting on their porches, we would stop and visit. However, my feet were itching to get to the end of the block where we would cross over the intersection into the king-size candy store, where you always had to stand in line and await your turn to choose your treat.

One hot, steamy Baltimore afternoon, Mother bathed and dressed me in a frilly dress. I went skipping out of the bedroom into the living room, turning circles, letting the skirt of my dress and my natural curly hair flow in the humid air. Granddaddy Ooking put aside his newspaper to smile at my excitement for life.

A tall man with large features, Granddaddy Ooking's face usually always had a reddish color from being outside at his lumber mill. His thinning, graying hair framed his gray-green eyes as he smiled and teased, "You look pretty enough to take to the candy store."

I had not turned three years of age yet, but somehow I had gotten this deep desire to walk to the store alone. I stood in front of Granddaddy and pleaded, "Let me walk to the candy store all by myself."

He put coins in my hand and asked, "Will you bring me some candy?"

Immediately, I went for the steps as if I had gone by myself many times. Once on the sidewalk, I walked slowly, swishing the skirt of my dress as I looked for neighbors sitting on their porches. Not only had I wanted to go alone but it also was important that the neighbors saw me walking to the candy store alone. The farther I walked by myself, the more disappointed I became; I saw no one.

When I got to the intersection, I watched both ways, just as I had promised, before crossing over to the store. Slowly, I opened the heavy door, entered the candy store, and made my way to the back of the line. I felt small standing behind the adults until I saw a girl about my size standing near and staring at me.

Suddenly, she began screaming, "Mother, Mother, this girl slapped me!" Everyone turned and looked back at us.

The girl's mother came, took her daughter by the hand, and told me, "Do not ever touch my daughter again."

For the first time, I had to figure out how to defend myself in the big world. I panicked and ran out the door as a customer entered. I ran across the intersection without looking. Back in the apartment, I stood before Granddad Ooking, tears running down my cheeks, and told him about the false accusation.

I felt protected holding Granddad's hand as we walked into the candy store, and he led me to the head of the line. There stood the little girl beside her mother holding a large brown bag of goodies. Granddad Ooking confronted the mother. "My granddaughter did not touch your daughter."

The mother said, "My daughter has been known to make up stories to try to trick me into buying her whatever she wants." Unknown to me, in just a few short months, I would live out the rest of my childhood under another woman and her daughter's tricks and false accusations, and there would be no one ever to intervene for me.

Also at that time, Adolf Hitler tricked surrounding European countries by proclaiming that he had no further interest in them when, in reality, he had plans to surprise, terrorize, incapacitate, and march in cities by his motto "Destroy by all and any means. National Socialism will reshape the world."

From the beginning of my life, I had watched adults sitting in front of floor-model radios, listening to the latest war news updates. This was how I first remembered meeting my dad. This man whom I had never seen before but somehow known as my father was in our apartment that night. After the evening news signed off, he lifted me up onto the couch and sat me upon his lap. In a soft, loving voice, he said, "I do not want you to ever forget what I am about to tell you."

Suddenly, sitting upon his lap as if it were a throne, I felt like a queen, and I smiled and replied, "Okay!"

He took me in his arms and whispered, "Do not ever forget that you will always be my little girl." Even though I did not understand that he and my mother had decided to integrate me into another family, my dad's words awakened a need in me. I had to hear those words again.

The next evening, Dad sat at the table, eating and listening to the war news. I climbed up in a big chair and began hinting, "Do you remember what you told me last night?"

He ignored me and kept right on staring at the radio, listening to Hitler's accomplishments of conquering small European countries. He never looked at me or repeated those "wonderful words" ever again. I never remembered ever seeing him again. Even though he disappeared out of my life, he left his footprint etched on my soul and created a deep desire to be told, "You belong."

At this time, news focused on Hitler's move toward Britain, and Granddad Ooking moved Mother and me back to the Appalachian Mountains to live with him and Grandmother. Just before turning three years of age, I started another life with Granddad Ooking and Grandmother while my mother returned to school and her social life.

Grandmother's style of dressing was more like the 1940s movie stars than the women in the small mountain area who wore typical homemade gingham housedresses and aprons. My grandmother looked glamorous in full-leg slacks with front pleats and a scarf tied around her colored blond hair as if she were ready to ride in a convertible.

Another memory I had of Grandmother was that she drove a large four-door 1940 Chrysler sedan. Whenever she went to do her chores, I would sit low in the front seat, where my eyes focused on her red fingernail polish as she steered the big old car—*thump, thump*—over the loose boards of the wooden overhead bridge to the west end of town.

The railroad, located about thirty feet underneath the bridge, employed 70 percent of the townsmen. After crossing over the bridge, I usually sat up on my legs to watch and listen to the activity as we passed through the corridor of Esso gas station, furniture stores, Farm Bureau, A&P, Western Auto, drugstores, barbershops, two movie theaters, many churches, and of course, the hub of town, G. C. Murphy's five-and-dime. Among these places were several storefronts of small family businesses, insurance companies, local newspaper companies, and boutique shops.

It hadn't been too many years since primitive life had consisted of a two-lane dirt road for Main Street and hitching posts for horses and wagons. Now some people drove their Ford, Chrysler, and Chevy vehicles on the busy asphalted streets mixed in with farmers' pickup trucks.

I knew we were headed back to the east end of town when I heard the tires thump on the overhead bridge. At the end of the bridge, Grandmother usually pulled over in front of the building supply shop Granddad Ooking had modernized from a small flour mill into the town's major building and farm machinery supplier.

Born in 1888 in a small nearby community, Granddad Ooking had worked as a freight conductor for the railroad. In work-related travels, he met Grandmother and married her in 1912. Six years later, he left his railroad position to open a flour mill. In just a few years, the need for grain to be ground decreased, with customers purchasing flour from supermarkets. Since he was from generations of lumbermen, he added a plane to dress lumber and changed the flour mill into a lumber mill. His business became a success to the point that, at the time of his death in 1960, Lowe's Lumber Company had purchased his store and, for the first time, began serving our town.

Grandmother let me run ahead of her into the building supply shop, where I loved to stand in the doorway soaking up the aroma of Granddad Ooking's King Edward cigars mixed with the smell of Beech-Nut chewing gum as he worked at the large old rolltop desk. After a short visit, Grandmother drove the two blocks home to begin preparing dinner.

Most evenings, I followed my granddad around the backyard, which was as picturesque as the garden in the movie *Secret Garden*. I loved walking among the assorted types and colors of rosebushes, tall flowers, gigantic trees, and rows of vegetables in the garden. However, my favorites were the window's flower boxes, and Granddad Ooking would lift me up high enough to water the flowers in the window boxes.

It was that spring when I remembered my first Easter. I awoke on Easter Sunday morning to find a sand bucket with pictures of bunnies on it sitting on a chair by my bed. I jumped out of bed to explore the funny bucket filled with funny green grass. After devouring the candy, I used the bucket to water the flowers and to shovel in the garden.

> On another day, the angels came to present themselves before the Lord, and Satan also came with them to present himself before him. And the Lord said to Satan, "Where have you come from?"
>
> Satan answered the Lord, "From roaming through the earth and going back and forth in it."
>
> Then the Lord said to Satan, "Have you considered my servant Job? There is no one on earth like him; he is blameless and upright, a man who fears God and shuns evil. And he still maintains his integrity, though you incited me against him to ruin him without any reason."
>
> "Skin for skin!" Satan replied. "A man will give all he has for his own life. But stretch out your hand and strike his flesh and bones, and he will surely curse you to your face."
>
> The Lord said to Satan, "Very well, then, he is in your hands; but you must spare his life." (Job 2:3–6)

While I was living with my grandparents, one afternoon, their only son, Ben; his wife; and three children came to visit. The prearranged setting for the visit was for my mother to be sitting under a large tree in the backyard when the family arrived. This would be my introduction to Uncle Ben and Aunt Mary and their three children, Steve, John, and Susie; and they only lived four blocks away.

The adults went inside the house to talk and left my mother to acquaint me with the cousins. She began by reading a story I had heard many times, and I became bored and went into the house. The first thing I noticed as I entered the kitchen was that the dinner dishes were still sitting on the table and that a dark liquid was in a glass. Thinking it was Coke, I turned it up and gulped it down; and all at once, I began coughing, gagging, and screaming. This brought the adults from the living room and the cousins and my mother from under the tree in the backyard to the kitchen.

Grandmother cried, "Oh no, she drank shampoo!"

My mother ran for me with a look of concern on her face when Grandmother shouted, "No, Martha, let Mary take care of her." This woman, whom I had just met, lifted me up on her lap and began patting my back. When I saw the scary look on her face, I jumped down, ran, and hid until she left.

It was not long after that first meeting with my future family I lost another secure home because my grandparents, Mother, and I moved into an apartment over a man's clothing store on Main Street. Granddad sold the Victorian house before his new home on the west side of town was built, and this would be our holding place until its completion.

One day Uncle Ben arrived with his little girl, and Mother told me to show my little cousin Susie around the apartment while she talked with her brother.

However, I could not remember seeing Susie again until Granddaddy Ooking moved us into our sort of Cape Cod–style newly built home. Grandmother invited me to take Susie up to the dormer room to play while she talked with her son, Ben, about taking me into his family. The main reason was that my grandparents were sending my mother to a girl's finishing school (about seven hours from home). That fall, Grandmother had become exhausted trying to keep up with me.

I loved to play in the upstairs almost as much as I loved playing in the beautiful garden at the Victorian house. There were twin beds, a trunk, hatboxes, and adult clothing of different sizes and styles for Susie and me. Nevertheless, the glamorous life did not last when Uncle Ben agreed to take me into his home. As Hitler moved his hate war from Britain to Russia in America, my third move in less than three years took me into a war zone of hate.

In my secure and confident way, I got out of the car in front of a small, two-bedroom white-framed house, which stood behind a white picket fence. Self-assured in my fancy dress, patent shoes, and natural brown curls bouncing in the air, I walked through the gate of horror. As I passed, I did pause to look at the white wicker furniture, which Grandmother had given her son's family when she moved into the apartment.

Uncle Ben followed closely behind, reached, and opened the screen door. I entered the living room, strutted straight back to the dining room, and sashayed around to look in the kitchen. I could not believe my eyes. There sat Aunt Mary, and she gave me the same ugly look that she had given me when I drank shampoo. Only this time, I could not run from her ugly glances.

She sat on a tall stool with her legs under the sink, which hung on the wall, as if she were sitting at a desk. I saw that her arms were in suds up to her elbows, which made me laugh, which made her angry with me. She glared from under her long stringy dark hair, which hung loosely around her shoulders. Quickly, I dropped my eyes to see her white cotton slip hanging beneath a torn, shabby cotton dress. This time, when fear struck, not only did my stomach begin to hurt but I also became as stiff as a board when I heard her command, "Change your dress and help with the chores."

I did not know how to take off my frilly white dress. After a long pause, Bob, Mary's teenage brother, came to my rescue. He had come to live with his sister after a long-standing problem between their parents erupted. The seventeen-year-old Bob finished high school, worked at the building supply shop for Granddad Ooking, and lived here with his sister. The compassionate teenage boy instructed me how to take my dress off. It had to be because of the pain he felt as the youngest left home with trouble brewing between his parents, which led to a divorce in a time when divorce was hardly ever heard of.

Gently, Bob took my arms, crossed them to each side of the hem of my dress, and instructed, "Lift your arms and pull the dress up over your head." I could still feel how proud I felt when I successfully pulled that dress off over my head. Bob led me to the back bedroom behind the dining room and picked up a dingy dress with one of the sashes missing from the side. I had never seen such an ugly dress. I began crying as he taught me to pull the dress down over my head.

This time, when I entered the dining room, my eyes focused on the floor. I felt as ugly as the woman on the stool looked. As fate would have it, life would become more terrifying than wearing a shabby dress.

On December 7, 1941, at three years and three months of age, I was lying in bed, listening to the radio and the people talking all at once in the living room across the hall. Suddenly, the people began letting out screams and shouts, which brought me out of bed, and I ran across the hall. There stood adults and children around the floor-model radio shouting at one another. Mary, whom I now had to call "Mother," demanded, "Get back to bed."

I still had enough confidence to speak up. "But . . . what is wrong?"

She gave me that ugly glare and snapped, "You would not understand! Get back in bed!" My body stiffened, and I felt as if I floated back across the hall. There were two strange words that stuck in my mind from that night until I went to my first library—Pearl Harbor. I found a copy of the *New York Times* dated Monday, December 8, 1941, which read, "Japan Wars on U.S. and Britain, Makes Sudden Attack on Hawaii; Heavy Fighting at Sea Reported."

The same month of Pearl Harbor was my first remembrance of a Christmas. After sitting around the Christmas tree until dark, Mother said, "Santa cannot deliver your toys until you are in bed." The boys immediately jumped up and went to bed.

I replied, "I want to stay and look at the lights on the tree."

Little Susie began to whine, "I want to stay and watch the lights on the tree."

The two of us sat together in a large overstuffed chair in our little chenille robes, which Grandmother had given us, and continued watching the lights blink on the prettiest tree I had ever seen.

Finally, Mother tricked me when she asked, "Will you do me a favor?"

Happily, I answered, "Yes."

She continued. "Will you go lie down with Susie until she goes to sleep? And then you can come back and look at the tree."

I jumped up and took the toddler to bed, and we both fell asleep until Christmas morning. I was impressed with how slick she got Susie and me to bed.

I had arrived at my new home with rosy cheeks, two sparkling eyes, and a bush of natural curly brown hair and entirely free of the knowledge of evil. By my fourth birthday, I felt as if something terrible would happen every moment of every day. The sparkle had left my eyes, my bushy hair was unwashed, and my once-high-spirited childish excitement for life had vanished. Added to that, my body felt as if I had dragged a hundred-pound weight every time I moved. Instead of romping with the new siblings, I tried to become invisible by hiding, either going under the bed or being amid five-year-old John, four-year-old Steve, and two-year-old Susie. After being an only child for almost three years, instantly, I became the third of four.

Four small children were too much for Mary, so Granddad Ooking came to the rescue and did something unusual in the 1940s. He enrolled John, Steve, and me into a day nursery one block behind his building supply shop. I could recollect the nursery experience because, at nap time, every child would put a pill (hard candy) in his or her mouth, which was supposed to be held under the tongue. My brothers would fuss at me when they heard the crunching coming from my mouth. I tried to hold the candy under my tongue to please them, but I could not keep myself from eating it.

Because Granddad Ooking had easy access to me at the nursery school, his son, Ben, and Mary withdrew me. When Granddad Ooking knocked on the door to see me, Mary and her children stuffed me into the bathroom and held my mouth shut until the knocking ceased. Mary, tired of Granddaddy Ooking trying to take me back to his house, blackmailed him; and I became her open bank account. To accomplish this, I became her prisoner of war, and she sentenced me to solitary confinement.

At the end of the long, narrow backyard at the alley stood a large tree where John and Steve played. To the left of that old tree, in a white wooden coal shed larger than a doghouse, I became incarcerated. After my eyes adjusted to the blue-black darkness, the main thing in my favor was that no one had scared me with the bogeyman. Then the terrible shock of isolation became daily routine where, instead of lying on smelly sheets, I found my bed on sticky straw.

The days were long and stuffy, and not only did I see darkly but my hearing also became dull. The hours spent in that building would still haunt me today when I would hear the lonely sound of an airplane or a dog barking off in the distance. I looked forward to the hand that placed a dish of food in the doorway as if I were a dog in a doghouse.

When I had lived in the apartment in Baltimore with my real mother, occasionally, she served me breakfast in bed. Now I would take the dish of food someone placed in the coal house, recline on the straw, and pretend to be with my beautiful mother (who now had been crowned queen of her college).

On a sunny afternoon, a man took me from the darkness of the shed. Immediately, the bright sun burned my eyes, and I tried to shield them by putting my hands over them. The man opened a car door and pushed me into the backseat. As my sight began to focus, I recognized him as Ben, my new daddy. In the backseat were John, Steve, and Susie. Mother was sitting in the front seat, and we were in Granddaddy Ooking's car.

As I tried to scoot back in the seat, my eyes focused on my hurting legs. In the dark, I thought the straw pricked my leg, and now I saw large red sores. Surprised by the sight, I forgot fear and screamed, "Mary—I mean, Mother, look at my legs!"

She turned and gave me an evil look, which caused me to become silent. She shouted, "What?" I pointed to one leg. "They're just fall sores caused by too much heat. Sit back in that seat and be quiet." I squeezed back in the seat between my elder brothers and was comforted by the smell of King Edward's cigars and Beech-Nut gum in the upholstery.

My new dad borrowed his father's vehicle for special occasions. In our small community, the middle class was not as blessed with automobiles as the more affluent until in the late fifties. Therefore, the twenty miles to where Mama and Poppy raised their seven children might as well have been a hundred miles away if a family did not have transportation.

Not only did families not have cars but the average family also did not have a telephone, and if they did, it cost too much to call long-distance. Therefore, once every couple of years, Mother visited her brothers and sisters. One reason many people did not know what was going on in our home was that Mother lived a reclusive life, which included controlling two of her three children until her death.

After what seemed like a long trip, we arrived at the family reunion with Mother's siblings and both of her divorced parents. I liked the relatives, whom I had just met for the first time, and they made a big deal out of the sores on my legs. In fact, I loved Mama because she questioned her daughter Mary, "Are you treating those sores on that child's legs?" Mother shrugged and gave me that fearful glare, and I ran to sit in the corner of the dining room.

After the isolation of the coal house, even the rattling of dishes was music to my ears. Mother's sister, Emma, had me drooling as she spooned golden fruit cocktail in delicate stem glassware, and there was a large chocolate cake to go with it.

The traumatic new life totally depleted my memory of running and playing with children. After dinner, I did not realize the cousins gathered outside and chased one another through the open fields of the farmland. Instead, I climbed the steep steps to the loft and dove into a feather tick mattress. The feathers pricked my sore legs, and when I started to get up, I heard Mother and Emma talking as they came up the steps. They entered the room across the hall, and I heard them talking. "We are in big trouble if Daddy smells our cigarette smoke."

I loved that afternoon when everyone was talking and laughing at once, doors were opening and slamming, children were running in and out, men were rolling cigarettes, and women were rattling dishes as they washed and dried them. Finally, time came for the thirty-minute ride back home. My fears were realized when Daddy stopped in front of the little shed and returned me to the coal house.

Another thing I could remember about the stay in the coal house was that, occasionally, John took me from the hiding place and lifted me into his little red wagon beside Susie. As he pulled the wagon around the alley, I had to keep my hands over my eyes to keep the bright sunrays from burning them.

Finally, the fall chill became my rescuer and took me out of the dirty coal house. What I did not know was that Mother had gone to her family reunion to arrange for me to spend a week with her siblings.

The first visit was with Uncle Alfred; his wife, Sue; and their little girl, Sherry. They lived in a cute little white-framed house on a dairy farm. Early one morning, Sue very lovingly began dressing me to tour the dairy barn. She took me to the back porch, pointed to the path I would take, and told me, "If you hurry, you will make it to the barn in time to watch Alfred milk the cows." Aunt Sue encouraged me on my way by promising to stand at the back door until I made it safely to the barn.

Slowly, I began to make my way toward the barn, looking back to see if my aunt still watched from the door. Halfway between the house and the barn, I looked up and saw for the first time an African American, standing by a pole. I became frightened and did not want to walk past the pole, so I decided to take the shortcut over the hill. As I began ascending the mound, I heard my aunt from the house and my uncle from the barn screaming, "No, Ivy! No, Ivy!"

Fearful of the different-looking man, I kept my eyes on him as I climbed faster and faster when, suddenly, I began to feel my body sinking down into the hill. By that time, I had sunk past my waist. Uncle Alfred, Aunt Sue, and the African American pulled me out of the mound of cow manure! After spraying me down with a hose outside in the cold weather, my aunt carried my cold, smelly, nude body into the house for a hot bath and clean clothes.

Just as I began to relax with Uncle Alfred and Aunt Sue, I had to spend the next week with Aunt Emma and Uncle Ken. They lived in what we affectionately referred to as "the country" where Poppy and Mama had raised their large family. My aunt introduced pork loins with biscuits and gravy to me, and Uncle Ken had a talent for making children feel special and safe. I could still hear his laughter as he tried to teach me how to crack nuts with a hammer and pick the meat out of the shells. Just as I settled in and became comfortable with them, Aunt Emma turned me over to her brother Leo and his family.

Leo lived on a farm three more miles down the hard road. His wife, Pat; daughter Joy; and his mother-in-law placed three delicious hot meals a day on the long table with two long benches on each side. I loved the early mornings before daylight, listening to the opening and shutting of the squeaky screen door and the dipper hitting against the water bucket as water was being dipped into glasses. I loved the smell of the fire in the cookstove with the aroma of coffee flowing in the cool morning air. When I heard them say, "Breakfast is ready," I jumped out of bed to get to the biscuits, gravy, and home-canned sausage.

After a hearty breakfast, the happy-go-lucky Joy and I made a cozy dollhouse up against the back of the house and pretended to rock our dolls to sleep. I pretended to have to go to the outhouse, and when Joy heard the chickens squawking, she knew that I had gone looking for eggs and came for me because her parents had given her strict orders to keep me out of the chicken yard.

After long days of chores on the farm, the family gathered around the country table for a supper of beans, potatoes, and corn bread. When the evening chores were completed, the family gathered in the middle room, which would later serve as my aunt and uncle's bedroom, and listened to war news on the radio while I brushed my aunt Emma's dark hair.

The week ended much too fast. I cried real tears when my uncle drove me in his 1938 Ford truck down the hard road to his eldest sister's house.

Aunt Mona's soft voice, gentle words, and hymn singing reminded me of Mama, her mother. Every evening, my uncle would come home from work carrying a small brown bag with the top twisted. I waited on the porch until I saw him coming, and I would take off running to meet him. I knew he had brought peppermint sticks.

After days of running barefoot through the beautiful wide-open green fields and gorges with newfound cousins, I departed for the fifth and final stop of the tour farther down the hard road where I met Aunt Betsy, Uncle Clarence, and their two-year-old daughter, Barb. This family did not live on a farm like the other family members but in the back of a grocery store where the backyard sloped down into New River. By now, over four years of age, my heart screamed for my real mother and Granddaddy Ooking to take care of me as I watched Aunt Betsy brush her little girl's long hair.

One day Aunt Betsy asked, "Ivy, if I watch you, will you walk up the side of the building and go in the front door of the store to buy me an onion?"

I felt proud as I climbed the long steep hill to the store, only I had never heard the word *onion*, so I pronounced to the store clerk, "My aunt wants a *youn-gun*." After repeating *youn-gun* several times, he sent me back to get a note from my aunt!

I loved the time after dinner because I would run down the sloping backyard as fast as my little legs could carry me toward New River, and I knew my uncle would catch me if I could not stop before going into the river. One evening while running down the hill, my finger began throbbing, and I began screaming. I did not remember that I had a ring on my finger until Uncle Clarence tried to take it off. The pain intensified as he pulled my finger and took a work file to cut the ring off the swollen finger. When he handed me the damaged gold ring with the letter *D* printed on it, I remembered Granddad Ooking putting the ring on my finger, and I began crying. I wanted my granddaddy Ooking. I did not know how to tell my uncle why I cried; he thought it was because the ring was broken.

No one in the family had any idea what manner of life I lived. In fact, the relatives thought of Mother and Daddy as well-off and felt inferior to them as they were farm people.

At the end of the visit, Uncle Clarence drove me back up the hard road toward town. When he stopped the car and opened the door, my heart sank. I got out in front of the white house sitting behind the white picket fence. However, this time, I did not notice the wicker furniture on the porch as I entered the house of the woman I had to call *Mother*. The first time I entered there was as a prissy little girl with a fancy frilly white dress. Sadly, I entered the second time as a withdrawn little girl and in desperate need of help. However, life had been mild compared to what lay ahead.

As fate would have it, upon my return, Steve and I came down with chicken pox. I lay with my head on top of the bed and he at the bottom, and whenever our feet touched, I screamed from fear that something would hurt me. My brother would tease, "That is chicken pecking your feet because you have chicken pox."

I would scream louder, "Get the chickens off my feet!" and the family would laugh.

One night, Granddad Ooking entered the bedroom. He gently asked, "Ivy, where is your candy?"

For the first time, I noticed the other children licking on peanut bars, and John refused to give me one of the five he held in his hand. After unsuccessful attempts, Granddaddy asked, "Would you give me one?"

John ran and handed him a bar of candy, and in turn, Granddad handed it to me. As impressed as I had been when Mother tricked me into bed at Christmas, in my childish mind, I was equally impressed by the way Granddad Ooking's trick worked to get me a bar of candy.

I became unaware of my body and lived in my thought processes. I began noticing that when John and Steve tormented me, they looked to their mother for her approval. My life, minute by minute, had become so uncertain in a strange world that I walked around like a zombie, and this came across as laughable rather than scary. The endurance in the coal house, compared to what the next big lesson was to be, seemed like child's play. I would suffer physical, mental, and spiritual abuse before the end of World War II.

I had become an expert at staying out of sight by crawling under the bed to play with the cans of food stored there. One night, Susie joined me to stack cans and topple them over, and Daddy entered the bedroom. When he lay on the bed, Mother entered, and I remembered my body becoming stiff when I heard Daddy shout, "Ivy, come up here!"

I feared the 250-pound man who wore a wide leather belt around his rounded waist, and I knew he would use it on me if I did not obey! My mind demanded my body to run, but as I stood by the bed, he demanded, "Lie down beside us." The large man's overwhelming power drew me, and I relinquished my power of resistance to his commands.

Unbelievably, at preschool age, I instinctively thought, *No! Please, no! This is wrong!* Once my stiff body lay down for the first time, I experienced the emotion of hate. Just to keep him from taking off his belt, I looked straight over their heads and dreamed of being with Granddad Ooking. Not until I began crying did he agree to let me go back to play. Once back under the bed, I rolled up in a ball, and my body shook.

The next surprise attack of my war happened on a sunny afternoon when I heard Mother call, "Ivy." I pretended not to hear her as I continued watching John lift the heavy trapdoor on the back porch floor to the dirt basement floor. He amused me by waiting until the rats were on the top step before dropping the lid on them.

Mother shouted my name again, and I shouted back, "What!"

She screamed, "Do not ask what! When I call you, come to see what I want!"

I walked slowly through the kitchen and dining room to the back bedroom door, stood outside the door, and bellowed, "What?"

She shouted, "Get in here!"

In desperation, I screamed, "What?"

"Come in here this minute," she snapped.

Slowly, I took hold of the doorknob and pushed the door open; and immediately, my body went limp. The odor made me feel sick and dirty. The dark green wartime window shades were pulled down, which made the dimly lit room scary. I became even more frightened when I saw Mother and Daddy standing in the middle of the floor with their arms wrapped around each other. Both of them gave me ugly smiles. I did not understand what they were doing, but I felt dirty and dropped my head. When Daddy demanded, "Look at us," again, the fear of his belt wrapping around my little body caused me to look straight ahead.

That day, I discovered that I could stare ahead, cry, and go into my fantasy world of children happily playing. Mother interrupted the fantasy by saying, "I get sick and tired of hearing you cry. Get out of here and make us a pot of coffee."

Happily, I turned, ran from the room, and slammed the door. However, I learned that day not to slam a door because Mother called me back to instruct, "Shut the door again, only this time, quietly."

Since I had never worked in a kitchen, I climbed on a chair and opened cabinet doors. Tears began dripping from my eyes; I knew Daddy would whip me with his belt if I did not bring coffee to them. Suddenly, I felt a hand on my shoulder. My eldest brother had climbed up on the chair with me to ask, "What are you doing up here?"

I said, "I am supposed to make coffee, and I do not know what that is."

He took a red bag of A&P Eight O'Clock Coffee from the shelf, taught me to measure water and coffee, and put the pot on a burner to perk. I stood watching him and thinking, *He is as smart as Uncle Bob, who taught me how to take off my dress.*

After I carried the coffee into the dingy bedroom, Mother warned me, "The next time I tell you to do something, you do it, and do not ask help from the boys."

When my brothers and I were left to ourselves, we had fun rolling down the grassy green hill between our house and the neighbor's, like in the story of the three little pigs in a barrel, which Granddad Ooking had read to me. One of our games backfired when we got in the car and were taking turns at the steering wheel. Even little Susie took a turn before me. I stood on the seat turning the big steering wheel the way I had watched Grandmother did with her red fingernails. Unexpectedly, Daddy appeared at the front door and shouted, "All of you children get out of that car and get in the house this minute!"

In the living room, he put me at the head of the line, and I watched with fear and trembling as he removed his leather belt from around his trousers. He raised the belt, and I screamed before it hit. Once it struck, I screamed even louder. He pointed to the bedroom across from the living room and told me, "Get in there!"

After he whipped my brothers and Susie, they entered the bedroom screaming real tears. I snickered, "Goody, goody, mine didn't hurt as much as yours."

Then I heard those terrible words. "Ivy, I heard that! Get back over here."

I watched for an instant as the big man took off the belt once more from around his waist and wrapped it around my little legs, and I ran back to the others screaming real tears. One thing was for sure: the smidgen of confidence I still possessed died with the sting of the belt and my siblings laughing at me when I reentered the bedroom.

Just before I turned five in the summer of 1943, I learned another lesson, naturally, the hard way. Mother trained me to hand laundry pieces from the basket as she pinned them to the line. Once the clothes dried, she folded them, and I had to lay them in the basket. At other times, I would entertain little Susie.

One hot June afternoon while I was playing with Susie, I missed my big brothers and periodically ran to the corner of the house looking for them. The last time I slipped off from Susie, I saw them leaning against the side of the house. Happy to see them, I ran closer and saw them trying to hide a pack of Camel cigarettes. I screamed, "I am going to tell Mother you are smoking!"

They begged, "No, Ivy, no!"

I turned and ran to Mother, shouting, "John and Steve are smoking!"

The boys followed close behind, crying, "Ivy ruins everything. Mother, we slipped off to the grocery to buy you cigarettes for your birthday, and she has ruined the surprise."

Mother wanted to know where they got the money. They both confessed they had stolen it from the grocery money in the china cabinet, and she laughed. She just patted her two sons on the head for trying to surprise her for her birthday. She promised the boys, "Because Ivy spoiled your surprise, we will not celebrate her birthday."

The only celebration I could remember on that long hot August birthday was when my brothers and I were chasing one another around the house. Finally, they decided to split up and trap me. They ran in opposite directions around the house, and the three of us were running so fast that we crashed into one another. Mother came running when she heard her two sons loudly screaming. She took care of them and left me sitting on the ground. I heard her say, "When are you boys going to learn to stay away from that troublemaker, Dumb Ivy?" Still sitting in the grass, I heard that horrible name for the first time, and it stung worse than bumping heads with my brothers.

They took their mother's warning seriously. The long hot days of summer became lonely as I sat in the wicker rocker, rocking the doll Granddad Ooking had given me. I decided that the best way to stay out of trouble was to not speak or play with anyone. However, the new name that Mother had given me gave my brothers a new way to tease me by coming to the side of the porch and singing the jingle, "Dumb Ivy can't catch us. Dumb Ivy can't catch us."

The birth of "Dumb Ivy" caused me to go deeper into myself and become despondent. I thought someone *did* care the afternoon Aunt Emma walked up the front porch and said, "Hello, Ivy."

I did not bat an eye. When she entered through the screen door, I heard my aunt inform her sister, "Something is badly wrong with Ivy. She acts as if she doesn't hear or see anyone."

As I listened, deep within myself, I cried, *Oh please, call me to join you*. However, it never happened in Mother's lifetime.

From that awful birthday without cake and ice cream and with the new nickname "Dumb Ivy," I began to live deeper within my thoughts. I became physically numb. In fact, I withdrew to the point I did not go in the house even to use the bathroom. I discovered that I could pull my little dirty cotton panties down, sit straight up in the grass with my dress over my legs, and urinate. Unbelievably, even sitting in the grass and not looking at anyone did not keep me out of trouble.

At noontime, I was sitting on my urine in the front yard when Uncle Bob arrived home from work for lunch. I asked him for a drink of water on his way into the house. After lunch, his sister walked him to the front porch and assured him that she would give me a drink. However, Mother turned, took her children into the house, and shut the door. The next thing I could remember was I had fallen forward over my doll and awakened to my brothers screaming, "Dumb Ivy killed our dog. If she hadn't left the gate open, the car would not have killed Blackie."

I had not moved from that spot since early morning. I looked through the slats of the white picket fence. My brothers were standing in the middle of the road and looking down at the dog. I could scarcely believe my ears when my brothers accused me of being a killer.

The last memories of living on Brown Street were just as bad as my first impression of the little white house behind the white picket fence. It was the night Granddad Ooking brightened the house with his visit. Susie and I happily poured clothespins onto the living room floor and began building a pigpen. She turned the round wooden pins one way, and I turned mine the opposite way to see how tall we could build the square pen without it falling. My brothers crawled across the hall and around the corner, knocked over our wooden pigpen, and crawled back across to the front bedroom. I began screaming, "John and Steve knocked over our pigpen!"

There was no way I could have known that Daddy and his father, Granddad Ooking, were having a serious conversation in the kitchen. Mother came into the living room, gave me one of her chilling glares that caused my stomach to begin swirling with butterflies, and promised, "After your granddad leaves, Daddy is going to whip you with the belt for this screaming."

Granddad Ooking had come to warn his son. "If you miss any more days of work, I will have to let you go."

As I slipped from the living room through the dining room to hide under the bed in the back bedroom (in hopes that Daddy would forget to whip me), I saw the two men in the kitchen. Granddaddy Ooking's face appeared white in color rather than his usual redness as he towered over the table, looking down at his son. The two men favored in that they both had piercing green-gray eyes and stood more than six feet tall, and their faces turned a bright red when they laughed. I loved those rare occasions when I saw the two men laughing together. This was not one of those times.

Fear gripped my stomach again when I heard the giant strides of my granddad walking through the house and the front door slamming. After the upsetting conference, Daddy came with Mother and his belt, dragged me out from under the bed, and released some of his anger on my defenseless body.

Out of stubbornness, anger, and pride, Daddy quit the only means he had of supporting his large family in his hometown. He would have to leave the poverty-stricken hometown and, for the first time, find work independent of his father.

Pres. Franklin D. Roosevelt had given the populace encouragement with the establishment of the New Deal. That program of relieving poverty proved not to be enough for the families in our area. The big government formed more committees to battle the results of the Depression, and more soup kitchens were established. The poverty level was such that needy people stood on street corners selling pencils and apples. As a young child, I saw individuals purchasing luscious red apples; and of course, I wished to find a nickel to purchase one.

As August 30, 1943, came and went in the middle of the poverty-stricken area, the issue of my fifth birthday did not include ice cream and cake as birthdays did for Mother's own children. When Mother and her sons made big issues of the leaders of World War II—Britain's genius Winston Churchill, Master Joe Stalin of Russia, our own general Dwight D. Eisenhower, and President Roosevelt—I assumed these men out of the radio were part of my kinfolk. When Eisenhower was appointed commander for the European invasion, I laughed every time Mother commented, "Lalala, I knew there would be another war. And President Roosevelt, Eisenhower, and Churchill are the only men who can handle Hitler."

On January 14, 1944, Uncle Bob celebrated his eighteenth birthday, and later a letter arrived from Uncle Sam, calling him to active duty. In addition, Daddy decided to do his part for the war by taking a job at Sparrows Point, a shipyard, in Baltimore, Maryland.

What World War II did for the depressed American economy, President Roosevelt's Works Progress Administration (WPA) could never have accomplished. The president requested industries to produce airplanes, jeeps, trucks, tanks, and ships. Many of our men were sent to Europe to fight against Hitler's takeover, and many women sacrificed home and family to work in the factories. The sacrifice our country made during the war efforts also caused shortages in food, clothing, and especially housing. Therefore, Granddad Ooking had no trouble selling our house before Dad could find us a place to live in Baltimore.

Granddad Ooking rented a one-bedroom apartment over the Farm Bureau on Main Street for Mother and her four children. This change in my life gave me a newfound freedom because there were fewer chores in the small apartment and no meals to prepare for Daddy and Uncle Bob three times a day. In addition, living in the apartment close to neighbors made Mother's demands ease up on me. Mother cared very much what others thought of her and protected her reputation at all costs.

Even so, I stayed in one kind of trouble or another. Anytime I did or said something wrong, I had to sit on the dunce stool in front of the kitchen window with a cake of soap in my mouth while my siblings laughed at me.

That fall, Steve began first grade at Nob School, and John began second grade. When I would sit in front of the second-story window in the kitchen, I would wish that we had a line to reel clothes out over the alley below, like the one in Baltimore when I lived with my real mother. Looking out the window, I felt as high as the sky as I waited to hear the ringing of the school bell. I looked forward to those warm spring days when my brothers got home from school and took me back with them to play on Nob School's playground.

Once out of the apartment, John led the march up on Main Street. At the second left, we turned and walked to the large brick building, which sat up on a knoll. When I saw the school, I ran ahead of the boys up the steep steps to scatter the blue jays, which were in the big old oak trees that lined the three landings of steps. John had to call me, "Come down the steps. We are going to the ball field." On the large dirt field, we could ride the merry-go-round, slide, seesaw, or swing on one of the three swings. I had long ago lost the ability to play, and I sat on a swing and watched my brothers play ball as if I were their mother.

At other times, Mother put John in charge of watching us children if we wanted to stand on the sidewalk at the doorway leading upstairs to our apartment. One boring Saturday afternoon, the two elder boys came up with a bright idea as we stood in the doorway. I was not smart enough to realize that when my brothers were nice to me, they were planning for me to do something bad. John said, "Ivy, see those two girls coming toward us with ice cream cones?"

My mouth began watering for the taste of ice cream. I gave him a big smile and replied, "Yes."

Steve joined in with John and said, "Grab one of the cones when the girls pass by." For the first time, my brothers really acted as if they wanted me to be part of their team, so I agreed.

The two boys and Susie went into the hallway to sit on the steps, and I took my place in front of the door. Just as the girls approached, I took a step forward and snatched a cone from the girl closest to me. Oh, the look of shock on the girls' faces as they began running away from me. I stood there feeling that the ice cream smashed in my hand would be a trophy to show my elder brothers. I felt proud when I heard them laughing from behind the door. They came out, and I asked, "How will I clean my hands before Mother sees me?"

John began looking up and down the street before he had a solution. "You see the woman coming with the black coat?"

Innocently, I nodded. "Yes."

He began laughing again. "Wipe your hand on her coat."

As the tall dark-headed woman came toward me, I stepped forward and wiped the vanilla ice cream on the side of her dark-colored coat. When I saw the anger on her face as she shook some of the mess from her coat before getting into the car parked nearby, I ran into the building to hear the praises from my brothers. They were laughing so hard that tears streamed down their faces, and I felt so proud of myself.

A few years later, Mother went to her grandmother's funeral. She returned home humiliated. Bernice, her cousin, had told her about the incident with the ice cream. She had been that woman! When she questioned us, the boys couldn't recount the events because they were rolling on the floor laughing. The scene pleased their mother, and she began laughing with them. I never heard another thing about it.

Another time, I created my own crisis when Mother sent me downstairs on my first assignment to the Farm Bureau. With my grocery list in hand, I walked in the door; and my eyes saw only the large barrels of brown sugar, candies, and nuts. I walked from barrel to barrel, sampling, while the clerk filled Mother's order. When he handed me a large brown grocery bag containing the items, I took a handful of nuts from a barrel on the way out the door. When I returned upstairs, Mother asked, "Where did you get those nuts?"

I replied, "The Farm Bureau."

She screamed, "Take them back downstairs this minute and tell the clerk that you stole them."

I felt ashamed and could not face the clerk. Instead, once outside, I walked around to the back of the building, found a large rock in the alley, and cracked the nuts the way my uncle had taught me.

When I returned back upstairs, Mother put me on the dunce stool by the kitchen window. When I heard the school bell ringing, I knew that in a matter of minutes I would get to go to the playground. Before John and Steve got the apartment door closed, I heard Mother begin, "You will not believe what Dumb Ivy did this time!"

After she recounted the events, the guys began singing, "Dumb Ivy is a thief," and they would not let me go outside with them.

I sat by the kitchen window crying when, suddenly, my brothers came bursting in the door, screaming, "Mother! Mother!"

I ran to the door to see what the excitement was about, and the boys were holding shells in their hands. "Mother, look at these shells we found in the alley! Dumb Ivy did not take the nuts back to the store."

I began backing toward the kitchen when Mother looked at me and said, "If it were not for the neighbors, I would beat you."

In May of 1944, just a month before school would be out for the summer, Daddy finally found a three-room apartment to rent in Baltimore with the promise of a two-bedroom government housing unit by the time school began in the fall.

The mustangs might have been escorting American bombers in daylight attacks in Germany, but our grandparents were escorting Mother and her four small children to the depot at the lower end of Main Street. We would ride the train to Washington, DC, and then change trains to Baltimore.

When we entered the overcrowded car with only a few seats available, Mother squeezed me in between two soldiers toward the back of the car. I felt secure as long as I could see Mother's and Susie's heads, with John and Steve in the seat in front of her.

Before Granddad Ooking got off the train, he asked me if I would be okay so far from the family. Mother interrupted, "I promise that I will move her up once everyone gets settled." Our grandparents kissed us good-bye and left the train.

After the eastbound train began moving, I went to sleep, squeezed between the two men, listening to the clanking of the wheels on the tracks. Hours later, arriving in Washington, DC, the soldiers gently stood me on my feet and led me to my family.

When we entered Union Station, we saw more people than those who lived in our small town. The four of us were holding close to Mother's coattail when we saw our first escalators. We could not understand how crowds of people were going up and down the steps without walking. Mother pulled us to a corner of the room and instructed, "John, do not let Susie out of your sight while I go stand in line for tickets to Baltimore." While we kept our eyes on Mother, unknown to us, Susie had wandered off to investigate the escalator.

Just as Mother turned from getting the tickets, she saw her little girl going up the escalator. She screamed, "John, you go up in the elevator, and I will take the escalator."

Steve and I began crying loudly, "We want our little sister."

Mother arrived to take little Susie off the moving steps before John got off the elevator. Mother gladly shoved all four of us onto the train to continue the last hour of the trip before meeting Daddy.

By the time the train pulled into the Baltimore station and remembering how Susie became separated from us, the four of us were very careful to stay close to Mother until I saw Dad waving from afar. I slowed and lagged behind while the family greeted him before getting in the car.

We had always lived in small houses for the size of the family, but oh, what confusion it was with four children and two adults crammed into three small rooms. Immediately, Mother—back to her old habits—went to the kitchen to make coffee and shouted, "Ivy, clean the bedroom and bathroom." As usual, I walked slowly toward the smelly bedroom where, immediately, I saw the stale chewing tobacco can on the floor, just like I remembered from back home.

After settling in, Mother made the big decision to send me to the last few weeks of first grade. I had never even been to school. Daddy took John and Steve on a trial walk to find the school, and the next morning, I followed the boys into the principal's office.

The second- and third-grade brothers handed the principal their transfer papers from Nob School and answered all the enrollment questions as if they were adults. When my turn came, the principal told my brothers, "Your sister will not be six until August, and she cannot start school until September. You will have to take her outside."

Tenderly, Steve took me by the shoulders as he said, "Ivy, you are not old enough to be in school, and I will take you to the playground."

We walked across the gigantic playground, about ten times larger than Nob School's. My concerned brother sat me on one of the short, fat posts that encircled the playground and told me, "Sit on this post and don't move until we come for you."

I thought that if I moved at all, he wouldn't be able to see me when he returned, so I sat as straight as I could until I became numb. Suddenly, in the heat of the morning, I heard a bell ringing. Steve came running out with a lot of children and waved at me. As he disappeared on the other side of the school building, I screamed, "Come back! I need to go to the bathroom! I am hot! I want a drink of water! I need to go to the bathroom."

During the long period of silence, I have no idea when or where I learned the song "Mary Had a Little Lamb," but the words became very real to me that long hot day in Baltimore. I actually believed that I was the lamb that followed my brothers to school and that the teacher turned me out. I sat on that post in the same position all day long. When my brothers came for me, they lifted me off the post; and with one on each side of me, they walked me home.

As soon as the door opened to the apartment, both brothers were explaining what happened to me at school. Mother never looked at me. She continued listening to the World War II news and shouted, "Dumb Ivy, get to your chores."

Before dawn on D-day, June 6, two hundred thousand men took part in the invasion of France. Britain defeated the Germans on the eastern sector of the beaches and captured war-torn Cannes, France.

During this period, Daddy trapped me in the second-floor apartment in a Baltimore heat wave.

Mother had taken an early-evening clerk's position at Read's Drugstore. She left for work when the boys got home from school, and before leaving for work, she placed pinto beans and potatoes in pots on the stove and ordered me to stay in the apartment and serve the family when Daddy arrived home from the shipyard.

I was two months away from being six years old, and it never dawned on me to disobey and sneak out to play. From the kitchen window, I watched my siblings and the neighborhood kids playing in the back alley until the time to serve dinner.

After dinner, Daddy insisted that the children go back outside while I did the dishes. Slowly, I climbed up on a chair, filled the dishpan with bubbles, and began to wash the dishes. Daddy sat in the living room, and I despised the way he stared at me from the couch. Ever so slowly, I washed the dried beans and potatoes from the pots as an excuse to linger.

However, when I stalled too long, he insisted that I not dry the dishes but leave them to drain. He called me to come and sit beside him. As stiff as a board, I walked to the living room, crying, and sat on the couch. I never sat close to him, but he would take my little arm and pull me close. Then he would either put one of my little fingers in his mouth or laid my hand near the zipper of his trousers. Instinctively, I knew it meant something wrong, and it felt horrible being near him! I hated him! I hated the smell of him! I hated his touch! I hated the frightening atmosphere in the apartment, which made me afraid to move one muscle!

Since coming to live with this family, I dealt with fear by going back in my mind to the wonderful, happy days with my real mother and Granddad Ooking. It took all my energy serving dinner and dreading the evening alone with Dad. I believed Dad became stimulated when he saw the terror in my eyes. I was completely under his power.

Occasionally, out of the silence came a knock echoing through the wall of fear, and there would be two girls about my age standing in the hall when Daddy opened the door. I loved the sound of their angelic voices. "Please let Ivy come out and play with us."

I made him furious by joining in, begging, "Please, Daddy, let me go please."

One evening tears streamed down my cheeks as I listened to him tell the girls, "Do not knock on the door again. When Ivy can play, she will be out."

I believed the neighbors heard me crying, "Daddy, no! Daddy, no!" The windows were open. They had to hear my cries, which sent those two angels to invite me out to play.

The few times that I did get to go out with the girls, Daddy had to see from the window that I never played with them. I did not know how to play. I sat on the grass like an elderly woman and watched the children play.

However, the last time Daddy gave me permission to go outside with the girls, I received a surprise, which was encouraging to me. I heard my name called from an apartment building that backed up to the alley straight across from ours. I looked up to the second-floor window and saw a handsome man and a pretty woman looking down at me. The woman smiled and asked, "Do you want to come up to our apartment?"

The first thought that entered my mind—but I did not know how to voice it—was *There are no doors to the back of your building, just windows.* However, I replied, "No."

The man got my attention when he replied, "We want to give you some candy."

I did not know what to say when the handsome man and the pretty woman told me, "Wait right there. We will be back."

They returned to the window with instructions. "You stand under the window, and we will send the candy down to you."

I watched as a small package was lowered down from their window on a string. I watched as the candy came lower and lower. Just before it reached the top of my head, other children began to gather, shouting, "I want candy!"

I heard Dad's voice. "Ivy, come in the house."

The couple was shouting, "Everyone, leave Ivy alone. She is special, and that candy belongs to her."

At dusk, my brothers came up to the apartment to listen to their favorite radio shows, singing, "Dumb Ivy would not share her candy."

Under the circumstances, I did not care what they sang or said to me. I needed their presence in the apartment. Usually, Dad would go to bed and leave us to listen to the radio.

There were certain programs that John and Steve would not miss, and no one better interrupt them. In the last two years of living with this new family, their bizarre behavior had me frightened during some of my brothers' shows. Organ music would fill the air with the Shadow's creepy laughter, followed by "Who knows what evil lurks in hearts of men?" After the laughter, before he answered himself, "The Shadow knows," that distressing voice and monstrous laugh would vibrate in my soul before fading into the program of "good fighting evil." The Phantom fought for good and struck terror in the very souls of criminals.

After *The Shadow* was another program called *Inner Sanctum Mysteries* with the sounds of a creaking door hinge. I knew that as seven- and eight-year-olds, my brothers had their own private wars and did not understand mine. Therefore, I irritated them by covering my head during these strange sounds.

The hard times in the apartment seemed nothing compared to the rough time ahead when we moved into the government projects at 1314 Gage Street. By this time, I had turned six years old. My brothers assured me that the teacher would not turn me out on the first day of school. However, the teacher *did* turn me out. She sent for my brother to take me home, along with a note for Mother, stating, "Do not send Ivy back to school until she has been vaccinated."

In my little world of horrors, the doctor insisted that he put the vaccination in my hip instead of my arm. He advised Mother, "The shot should go in your daughter's hip because it will leave a scar on her arm. That will not look nice when she grows up and wears an evening gown." Mother agreed with him. It took the nurse, Mother, and the doctor to hold me down while the doctor pulled down my panties with me screaming. After surviving the shot crisis, there would be another note from the teacher creating more disaster in my fragile life.

The influx of people in Baltimore during the war made it necessary to institute swing shifts to accommodate all schoolchildren. The note stated that I had been assigned to the early-morning shift before daylight. I became frozen with fear when I heard that Dad would drop me off at school since he worked the early shift at the shipyards.

The first morning, I got out of his car in the dark and opened the huge heavy school door. As I began the long walk down the narrow hallway, I looked up at the darkness through the windows that lined the upper part of the corridor. I felt as small as an atom, which no one could see. The worst part of all was that I had no idea why I went to school, and I walked down the hall as if in a fog. A teacher took my hand, led me to my first-grade classroom, and lifted me up into the first seat in the first row.

I felt relieved once settled in the big desk, where my feet did not touch the floor. I put my elbows on the desktop and propped up my head.

On the last hour of the day, combined classes were led to the music room, where I ran for a chair near the piano. My real mother had played the piano at Granddad Ooking's house.

Music was the only thing familiar to me at school, and I took learning the new songs very seriously, even when the top of my leg began to itch. I pulled up my cute little wool skirt, which Grandmother had given me, and began scratching. In my little world of nothingness, I had not been aware of other children until I heard the boy next to me shout, "Eew!"

Startled, I looked at him, and he was making a face at my leg. Instinctively, I reached over and pinched the top of his leg. He let out a bloodcurdling scream, "She pinched me! She pinched me!" just as the dismissal bell rang.

The teacher did not blame either of us and instructed, "You two keep your seats while the rest of the class is dismissed." After each student stared at the two of us while filing out of the room, the teacher continued. "I will not have you disrupting my class. You two children stay in your chairs until I say you can leave."

It seemed like hours of silence before I heard voices from a distance, shouting, "Ivy, Ivy, where are you?" John and Steve came rushing into the room out of breath. "Mother sent us to find you."

The teacher replied, "Your sister had a problem with another student and had to stay in after school."

When the teacher let me go, my brothers were infuriated because I had made them miss their radio shows. When we entered the house, they asked, "Mother, how did the radio show end?" Then they settled down for the next program after Mother assigned me double chores for causing trouble.

The next day of school, when the dismissal bell rang, I left the building with the other children. When they began dispersing in all directions, suddenly, I realized that I had never walked home alone. I did not know which way was home until I recognized the little boy who lived across the street from me.

By now, after so many weird happenings in my new home, a feeling had been instilled in me that it was dirty to be around the opposite sex. Therefore, I decided to hide behind one of the many large trees lining the blocks to follow my neighbor home. I ran from tree to tree, making sure I did not lose his trail home, and the boy stopped every other step to pick up treasures along the sidewalk.

Concentrating on staying well hidden behind the trees so he would not discover me, I did not hear the very angry John and Steve appear until they began shouting, "Why are you standing behind this tree?"

I explained as I pointed to the boy playing up ahead, "I didn't know the way home, and I was waiting to follow him."

I had to run fast to keep up with my fuming brothers. When we walked through the front door, my brothers told Mother, "She was playing with the boy across the street."

For the first time, Mother replied, "You just wait until your daddy gets home. He will whip you." That comment further instilled in me it was dirty to be with the opposite sex.

After dinner, I climbed up on the chair and lingered over cleaning the bean pot. Nevertheless, true to her word, I heard Mother call from her bedroom, "Ivy, get in here now."

When I entered the bedroom, Mother stood guarding the door, and Daddy began, "Why were you hiding behind the tree with a neighbor boy?"

Frustrated, I tried to defend myself. "I didn't know the way home." When he stood and took off his belt, I pleaded, "Please don't hit me! I didn't know the way home."

He folded the belt in half. "Crying will only make the whipping worse!" He repeatedly asked, "Why were you hiding behind a tree with a boy?"

I began screaming before the belt reached my little body each time. Once he had had enough, he threw me to the floor, and Mother dropped her dress and got under the covers with him. I walked out of the room to face my siblings.

After those belt strikes, I became fearful that Daddy would find out that Paul, the first little person whom I had ever seen wearing a round hat like Granddad Ooking, winked at me every time I turned around at school. The only time I had ever seen anyone wink was the day we were packing to move to Baltimore, and my aunt Emma sent me across a little side street to a café for candy. A man who looked like Daddy sat at the counter. He winked, and I automatically thought it was bad.

I never looked Paul in the face again, but from behind me, he would constantly whisper, "You are my girlfriend."

Between switching back and forth to school, chores, and World War II, Uncle Bob came for a ten-day furlough to our new home in Baltimore. When I got home from school, he demanded that I sit at the table beside him, and he began quizzing me about my name and address. As I watched him, he appeared to be angry with me until he began questioning his sister, "Mary, why would you send this child out in this big city without knowing her address? If she got lost, she could not even tell a policeman where she lives."

Bob used his ten-day furlough tutoring me in the alphabet, numbers, and my name and address. Before he left, I had learned everything except the letter that began my name. My uncle printed *D* on a piece of paper, pinned it to my dress, and throughout his furlough, he would point and say, "What is that letter?"

Not only did he open the world of learning but he also bought ice cream for the four of us whenever we heard the ringing of the bell on the ice cream truck. The day Uncle Bob picked up his duffel bag to leave, we sat on the doorstep screaming and crying, "Please don't leave us." When he arrived in France, the Germans trapped him and two other soldiers in a barn for ten days before they could escape and continue on to Germany.

Sometimes as Mother listened to the war news with my brothers, I would hear Daddy calling me. I would look at Mother, hoping she would tell me that I did not have to go. However, she ignored the silent pleas of my war.

The government housing projects had the same layout as the military housing, where each building was divided for four families with about a thousand square feet. At our end, the front door opened into the living room, which led to the kitchen and a small hall. From the hall, there were entrances into two bedrooms, and another horror would take place in the one bath in the middle of the house so the neighbor would not hear me.

However, this night, I walked slowly toward the little hall off the living room; turned right toward Daddy's bedroom, trying to keep one foot in the little hall; and peeked in his door. He demanded, "Come in here and shut the door."

Terrified, I felt as if I floated to his bed. I sat as far from him as I could and still be on the bed. When he did not reach out to touch me, I relaxed. He began, "Do you remember the last time we went to the country before moving here?"

Anytime we visited the relatives, it made me happy, and I smiled and mumbled, "Uh-hum."

He continued. "Do you remember going out to play?"

"Uh-huh!"

"Well . . ." He stopped for a minute before continuing. "Did you lie in the cornfield with your cousin?"

His surprising accusation of that event caused me to feel guilty for the first time in one of these sessions. He watched as I squirmed. I remembered my cousin shouting for me to come out in the field. He pointed for me to lie down between two rows of corn. I thought that was a funny game until I saw my cousin's hands coming toward my body, and I jumped up and ran back to the house.

He patiently asked the question again, "Did you lie in the cornfield?" I looked down at the floor and lied to him. He sat for what seemed like hours before standing.

Instead of going for the belt, he took two coins from his pocket. He smiled and teased, "Would you like these two quarters to buy ice cream?"

I smiled and answered, "Yes."

He repeated, "Did you lie in the cornfield?"

I looked down at the floor and whispered, "Yep." He put the two coins in my hand, I walked out of the bedroom, and his wife went in.

Back in the living room, I impressed my brothers when I held out my hand and whispered, "Look, I have two quarters for when the ice cream truck comes."

John figured we could buy two each. Steve suggested we buy one ice cream tonight and one the next night. All Susie knew was she wanted ice cream, and I knew I wanted everyone to like me.

While the four of us waited to hear the truck's bell, we happily sat on the living room floor talking when I heard something behind me. I turned, and there stood Mother holding out her hand for the money. With an ugly stare, she took the coins without speaking a word. When the little bell rang, we sat in total silence as other families ran to get in line for ice cream.

Daily, Mother sent her three children out to play with the other children in the neighborhood, while I had to be at her beck and call in the silent house. This frustration caused me to come up with another defense mechanism: volunteer to do chores, which I thought might keep me out of her bedroom.

One Saturday morning, the siblings were outside; and as usual, the parents were in their bedroom. To make sure they would not call me into their room, I began sweeping the kitchen floor as hard as I could. I swept under the stove, behind the refrigerator, and in every corner and made a large pile of rubbish. For the first time in my life, I attracted Mother's attention on purpose. I screamed, "Mother, will you come here?"

To my surprise, she came running. There in the kitchen doorway, I proudly displayed my trophy, which caused her to give me one of those looks as she turned to go back to the bedroom and shouted, "Do not sweep that mess out the front door."

I leaned over the pile, tried to coordinate the broom and dustpan, and swished up everything at once as I had seen her do. As everything slipped out of my small hands and went in all directions, I heard a voice from the door say, "It looks like you need help, young lady."

I looked, and there stood Aunt Betsy and Uncle Clarence with their six-month-old baby boy. Pleasantly surprised by the interruption, I ran to the door and asked, "Where is your baby, Barb?" I was disappointed when they told me she had stayed with relatives until they found work and an apartment.

This time, I screamed at the top of my lungs, "Mother, hurry and come here."

She ran to the living room with an outcry, "Stop it! I want you to stop—" Then she caught sight of her sister, grabbed the broom and dustpan, and in one big swoop handed me the dustpan full of rubbish to put in the trash can.

Jobs were plentiful in Baltimore during World War II, so Uncle Clarence found employment right away. Between him, Daddy, and Mother working different shifts, someone was getting up, going to bed, getting ready for work, cooking, or eating at all times. I loved the confusion and the activities that took the attention away from me. For the first time, I had freedom to roam the great outdoors.

Sitting alone in the green grass one bright, hot, sunny day, I discovered my first grasshopper, and I could not understand how those little things could spit tobacco juice just like Daddy. I tried to open its mouth to see the Brown's Mule tobacco, and it hopped away. I began looking in the grass for my new friend. To my surprise, I discovered many such creatures spitting around my legs.

During the short period of freedom, one night, my parents sat around the kitchen table talking with the relatives. John, the doctor, told me to pretend that I had an earache and come to his office for treatment. When he examined my ear, he gave me an uncooked pinto bean to put in my ear. Unknown to me, I was to pretend it was cotton and was not really supposed to put it in my ear, but I pushed it all the way in! Later, when the doctor asked for his piece of cotton back for the next patient, I cried, "But I can't get it out."

John ran into the kitchen, shouting, "Ivy has a bean in her ear!"

In the blackness of night, trembling, I climbed in the car with Daddy and drove to the doctor's office. When I saw the man in a white outfit come near me, I panicked, and Daddy held me in the chair while the doctor tried to flush the bean out with water. I screamed and bawled until the doctor told Daddy, "I cannot get hold of that bean."

I sat paralyzed in the dark car on the return trip home, alone with Daddy. The fear continued when we entered the house and I heard him shout, "Bring me a wartime bobby pin and not one of those new ones with a rubber tip." Mother and John held me in the kitchen chair while Daddy stuck the bobby pin's sharp metal tip in my ear and pulled out the swollen bean.

Unfortunately, my freedom ceased, the war escalated, and Clarence moved his little family to an apartment in Curtis Bay. Occasionally, Mother took me with her to visit Betsy. I loved going because every time I ran up the steep steps of the brick apartment building, it reminded me of running up the ones at Nob School.

I happily played on the steps with the neighborhood children, and we always kept an eye out for the candy man to appear with his tin of goodies. Along with the housing shortage, many items were rationed, including gasoline, rubber, cigarettes, and sugar. Not only did the adults have allocations but the more fortunate children also felt the shortage of bubble gum and candy. The white-headed man with a gentle smile would come up the steps and hold out the container for all the children to choose one piece of candy. We would squeal with delight for a piece of candy. He would turn, walk back down the steps, and disappear.

Usually after visiting, Betsy would push the baby in his stroller and stand in long lines with Mother and me to purchase ration items. We took our places about a block away and listened as people shared their concerns that the items they wanted would be gone by their turn. Mother held the ration stamps and hoped that she would get her quota of Camel cigarettes. Afterward, Mother and I continued along the sidewalk to the streetcar stop.

On the way, I would look down into the windows of the stores below the sidewalk, especially the good-smelling bakery. One time, we went into the bakery. I slipped back out the door to play on the sidewalk when I heard a dog bark. I lay on the sidewalk, looked back down the bakery, and saw the dog inside. I barked back at him. When Mother saw me, for the first time, she gave me an approving look. Even when we returned home, I felt proud as she told my brothers about the incident and ended the story with "And everyone in the bakery was laughing at Ivy and the dog barking at each other."

I became even more encouraged when, one spring day, Mother took me to the neighborhood market and handed me a square box with pictures of eggs and bunnies on both sides. She instructed, "When we get home, I will teach you how to color eggs for Easter."

I felt proud when she volunteered to let me carry the colorful box in one hand and a bag of groceries in the other. I followed her as we began the steep climb up the hill to our home. Suddenly, the wind began blowing violently and pushed me back down the hill. Turning and backing up the hill, Mother shouted, "You'd better put the egg kit in the bag, or it will blow away." At that instant, the wind pulled the kit from my hand, and it disappeared. I could not believe the words I heard come out of her mouth: "I am sorry the wind took the kit. I will hurry home and send John to help with the bag."

The next day, Mother continued her kindness by volunteering to let me go home with Betsy and stated, "After dinner tonight, we will come for you."

Soon after arriving at my aunt's apartment, I heard a knock at the door; and to my pleasant surprise, there stood candy man. There were no fast-food restaurants in those days, so men who had come to work in the shipyards, leaving their families back in hometowns, hired homemakers to cook them a meal and pack their lunches.

After candy man finished eating his lunch, I asked for a piece of candy, and the kind man told Aunt Betsy, "Since I am off from work tonight, I will go get the tin."

I pleaded with my aunt, "Please let me go with him." She only gave her approval after the couple who lived upstairs came to take the baby for a stroll and gave her a minute to relax. I held candy man's hand and skipped down the sidewalk as if I were with Granddaddy Ooking. He opened his apartment door and reached his arm in for the tin, and we were on our way back to my aunt's apartment.

True to her word, that evening, Mother and the whole family arrived. I began bragging about candy man, but my brothers did not believe me. John asked Mother, "Can we go with Ivy to visit her friend?"

It shocked all of us when she replied, "Yes, and you can stay until we come for you."

It also surprised candy man when he opened his apartment door to hear four children talking at once, "Our mother told us we could come to visit." Being a gracious man, he invited us into his apartment. We sat on the floor around his chair, and he began to read us a story. I lost interest and began exploring his small apartment.

On his dresser in the bedroom, I found what looked like the kind of combs that Grandmother wore in her hair, and I tried to stick them in my thick, curly hair. When they would not stay, frustrated, I went into the living room and told the kind man my problem. He replied, "Those are not hair combs. They are my false teeth."

Unbelievably, as I stood there holding the teeth, Daddy and Mother came for us. All Mother had to do was give me one of those ugly looks, and I put the teeth back where I found them. I thought it unusual for my parents to be visiting, especially with a man they had never met. However, there they sat laughing and talking with my friend as if they had known him for years. Finally, Mother and Dad gathered us to leave, and the man opened the tin box. Each one of us selected a piece of candy, and I smiled at my brothers in a manner of saying, "Ha ha, I told you he had candy."

I sat on the edge of the backseat, sucker in mouth, talking as fast as I could about the events of the day. Mother shouted, "Dumb Ivy, you do not have anything to be excited about. Sit back in that seat and be quiet." Quickly, I leaned back in the seat and continued wondering how that man got all his teeth out of his mouth.

When we entered the house, Mother told me, "Sit on the couch and do not move." Since the couch was where Susie and I slept, I could not understand why she took my sister into the boy's room. By now, I had become good at sensing the atmosphere. I felt tension in the air, and my body began an internal quivering while my sister was tucked into bed with her brothers.

Then I heard those dreadful words. "Ivy, come here." For a brief moment, I was too disoriented to move. I had to force my body to stand. My legs became rubbery, and I thought they would fold under me as I walked toward my parents' bedroom. I began chilling; Mother pulled me into the room, shut the door, and ordered me to get in bed with Daddy.

Psychologically paralyzed, I went to him. The former all-star football player reached out and lifted my body over his large frame to lie near the wall. I lay cowering, and nothing appeared real, as I had no power and no protection. I felt disconnected from my body as Dad's large frame rolled over to the right as if he would lie on top of me. He was propped up on his right elbow, the other hand rubbing my chest. I grabbed the skin under his left arm and began squeezing as a last-ditch effort to protect myself. He didn't act as if he felt my pinch.

The next thing I remembered, Dad lifted my little limp body, and Mother carried me through the hallway into my brothers' bedroom. When she laid me at the foot of one of the two full-size beds, it seemed as though all sounds were hushed and time and movement were no more.

I looked over my shoulder and saw Susie and Steve snuggled up, fast asleep. On the other side of the room, John was safely fast asleep in the other bed. Suddenly, the ugly woman demanded that I lift my legs so she could wash my feet. Weakly and slowly, I stuck my two helpless legs in the air. She was not interested in washing my feet but in awaking the children.

In further humiliation, instead of washing my feet, she spread my legs apart; and as if she were a distraught mother, she screamed loudly, "You are split open and bleeding! Daddy will have to take you to the hospital." She succeeded in waking the children as witnesses to the fact that she only discovered I had been raped when she went to wash my feet.

Dad's large hands picked me up as if he carried a rag doll, and took me out into the scary dark night. Incomprehensibly, I looked up from a hospital gurney into a circle of faces surrounding my bed, some in blue police uniforms and others in white medical uniforms. I thought I must have gotten lost because, on his furlough, Uncle Bob had told Mother, "Ivy needs to know her name and address in case she gets lost, so she could tell a policeman where she lives."

While I was still on the gurney, Daddy took a police officer to Aunt Betsy's apartment and asked for directions to the candy man's apartment, where our whole family had been that night. When my aunt asked the police officer, "What has happened?"

The officer told her, "Ivy is a frightened child, and there is evidence that she has been drugged by a shot in her arm before being raped." They left my aunt blaming herself for not protecting me while I was in her care. It would be forty-five years before she would learn the truth.

The next morning, Daddy and I climbed the steep steps into a large building, and I had to jog to keep up with him and a police officer walking down a long, wide corridor. The only sounds were their shoes pounding on the tile floor. We went down the steps and passed through a security door, which clanged shut behind us.

When we reached the end of a gray corridor, the officer stopped and motioned for me. I was unprepared to see candy man sitting on a steel slab in a dingy cell and behind bars. I stared at my friend. The sight of the brokenhearted man brought me to the brink of tears, and the police officer asked me several questions. There was no way at six years of age that I could have connected this with the night my dad raped me.

In addition, I did not understand the line of questions from the police. All I did was stand there wondering why my friend was in an animal cage. Finally, when I did not speak, the police officer assumed that I was afraid of the man behind bars and escorted Dad and me back upstairs.

Once home, I was convinced that I would have never remembered the jail if my two brothers had not been impressed that I had seen a real jail and sung repeatedly, "Dumb Ivy has seen a real jail."

At the time, I did not know what the word *jail* meant, but I knew it had something to do with the strange happenings in my fragile life. So I began crying out, "Mother, please make them stop singing."

A miracle happened: she did! To put it mildly, my parents were in a frenzy because I had not implicated candy man, and they decided to brainwash me. Their actions threatened to destroy my mental and physical being when they insisted that I give them details on how the man had raped me. Dad told his wife, "The bathroom is without a common wall with the neighbors. Put Ivy in there on a table." This was where the brainwashing was to take place.

After I finished the nightly dishes, I heard the dreaded words. "Ivy, get in the bathroom." When I entered the room, Dad lifted me up on the table, and the long hours of interrogation began. Once they started, if siblings came in the house to use the bathroom, I had the added humiliation of climbing off, facing my brothers, and standing in the hall until they used the bathroom.

The neighbors had to be hard of hearing not to hear my wild screams night after night! For hours, my movements were restrained while a man and woman stood on each side of me, repeating the same question every night, "What did the man take out of his pants?"

I repeated night after night, "Money."

At that word, Daddy wrapped his wide leather belt around my body for giving the wrong answer. The blows caused shrieks and howls as if I were an injured animal. No amount of torture would have given me the right answers to their brainwashing that the candy man had taken his penis out of his pants and raped me, even if he had.

Before the sessions ended, I would pass out from exhaustion and wake in the darkness of the bathroom long after my parents had gone to bed. I tried turning my sore body on the hard table, but I felt as if I weighed tons. To add to this confusion, there were nights when shattering sounds of air-raid sirens filled the bathroom, shattering my nerves. The fear actually made my body feel as cold and heavy as iron. I calmed myself by thinking, *If I lie straight and not move one part of my body, no one will hurt me.*

One morning days later, Mother took me from the bathroom table to the kitchen table. After breakfast, Daddy and I, once again, climbed the steps into the municipal building. This time, to add to the confusion of my mental state, I stood before a magistrate when the candy man walked in and sat at a table. The magistrate pointed to the sad, falsely accused man and asked me, "Do you know this man?"

The nights of beatings had numbed my thoughts, not to mention my body, and I could have never connected the dots of events in the last two weeks. I just stood with my head down. Every time the judge asked me a question, Daddy would be standing behind me, taking the toe of his shoe and tapping the heel of my shoe, prompting me to say that the candy man raped me. When I did not answer the magistrate's questions, I knew that meant the belt when Dad got me home.

The magistrate again pointed to my good friend and asked me, "Did this man hurt you?"

Again, I felt the toe tapping on my heel, and I did not lift up my head or speak a word. Finally, the court decided, "Take the man out of the room because the little girl is afraid of him." However, since I did not speak in court, I learned twenty years later that the innocent candy man went free, except for his reputation.

When we left the hearing, I took one look at Dad's face, and I knew more trouble lay ahead. To further brainwash me as to who raped me, he drove around Baltimore after the hearing and said, "When you see the building where the man who hurt you lives, let me know."

In a few minutes he snapped, "Now I am going to drive around the block one more time, and I want you to tell me where the man who hurt you lives." Sitting low in the car, all I could see were tops of buildings. I would do anything to keep him from taking his belt off, so I pointed at the first tall building I could see.

Dad immediately pulled over to the curb and threw me off guard by asking, "What is the man's name?"

Gasping for breath and thinking as fast as possible under the circumstances, I shouted the first name that came to mind, which was that of my uncle who taught me how to take my dress off and brush my hair, "Uncle Bob!"

Dad asked, "What is his last name?" The only last name I knew was ours, so I shouted that, and he got out of the car and disappeared into the building.

As I waited in the car, fear seized my body because I knew I had lied to him about the man's name. I saw him walking back toward the car. He got in, started the engine, and pulled away from the curb. Nothing! Not one word! For the first time in three years of living with this violent man, I had the audacity to ask, "Did you find him?"

He replied, "The name wasn't on the mailboxes." That was all! To him, that was the end of the brainwashing concerning the rape! Little did he understand that he had destroyed the lives of the candy man and my aunt Betsy and the innocence of a six-year-old child.

However, it did appear over the years that both of my parents were hoping someone would kidnap me. The first incident that I remembered was putting me on the train so far from the family. The second was sending me to school without my knowing the way home or my address. But one thing was for sure: Mother and Daddy understood how to benefit from their actions and take advantage of any situation.

After that day of the hearing, Dad disappeared; and in his absence, Mother darkened the house by pulling the green wartime window shades and kept not just me but also all her children locked in the dark house. During his absence, Mother had no money; and the day that we split the last slice of bread among us, we kids cried with Mother.

Days later, Dad returned, and his parents mysteriously arrived at our doorstep. They arrived because Dad went to them to tell them that I had been raped in the big city. He knew they would want to get me out of the city where that happened and would give him his job back at the building supply shop in our small hometown.

The first thing Granddad Ooking did upon his arrival was to flag down the milk truck and then the bread truck and purchase quarts of chocolate milk and chocolate-covered doughnuts and breads. The four of us ate, drank, and laughed until our grandparents departed.

I used to feel fresh, clean, and pretty in the presence of my grandparents. In just three short years, I felt dirty, and they could not understand why I avoided them. I feared my parents to the point that I would not even hug my grandparents. What they did not realize was that, deep in my heart, I wanted them to protect me; and oh, how soothing it was to smell the aroma of my granddaddy's King Edward cigar and Beech-Nut chewing gum.

The night I realized my grandparents were leaving, I slipped out the door and squeezed under the small low front porch. The thought of my grandparents touching me in front of my parents sent me into a tailspin. I heard my loving granddaddy say, "What happened to Ivy? I do not want to leave without kissing her good-bye."

From under the porch, I silently pleaded with him, *Do not say* kiss *in front of my parents, or they will whip me.* Tears dropped from my eyes onto the dirt when Granddad stepped off the porch. Then there was the sound of the car door shutting, and my heart was breaking.

After missing twenty-one days of first grade, I returned to school and wore one of the two plaid skirts Grandmother had given me. In my mental state, I did not listen to the teacher, nor was I conscious of the other students. I used the schooltime to relax, until I saw a dirty spot on my skirt. Since the rape, I hated to be dirty, so I began crying. When the teacher asked, "What is wrong?"

I did not want to tell her my skirt was dirty, so I lied, "I was sick last night, and Mother had to take me to the doctor."

On April 12, 1945, Mother heard the news flash that President Roosevelt had died. She cried! The tragic news shifted the focus from me to Harry S. Truman. Mother had become convinced that he was too inexperienced in foreign affairs and that this would hinder the United States from ending World War II anytime soon. However, on May 7, an unconditional surrender was signed at Eisenhower's headquarters in Reims, France.

On May 8, Victory in Europe (V-E) Day declared Hitler and Mussolini both dead. Thousands of people celebrated around the world, and it began one of the longest ice cream feasts of my life. As soldiers began arriving home over the next few weeks, anytime the bell rang, a soldier treated the whole neighborhood with ice cream. At times, I sat on the curb watching men in uniform sneak up on the porch and knock on their doors. Oh, how I loved the happy scenes of women and children running out of the door, screaming for joy as they gathered their loved one in their arms. Then when the ice cream bell rang, the soldier would gather all the children in the neighborhood.

After the emotional homecomings ended, I hated the scenes of families embracing for another farewell to arms. Every time a man let go of his family, he would grab his duffel bag and begin running down the street. I cried along with his family long after he had disappeared.

During those days of celebrations, Aunt Betsy would come to visit. I stood on a chair washing dishes, and I heard her shout, "I see Uncle Bob coming over the hill." I jumped down and ran out the door without permission, and there he came, walking over the same hill where I had lost my Easter egg kit.

John and Steve ran to carry his duffel bag. At first, I did not recognize my beloved uncle with a beard. Everyone held on to every word as he reported the horrible experience of how a German soldier had him at gunpoint when the news came that the war had ended in Europe.

I felt important that I had a relative who would treat the neighborhood children, as their parents had treated me, with ice cream. I thought the soldiers were the richest people in the world when they took out their wallets and paid for all that ice cream.

My relaxation, excitement, and celebration ended in chaos late one afternoon while sitting on the curb, eating ice cream with the neighborhood children. Daddy parked the shiny new dump truck that he had driven back from his dad's building supply shop in front of our house. Later that evening, the men put a mattress on the back, along with our few clothes. Then Uncle Bob lifted me into the back of the truck where I lay on the mattress and looked up at the tarp that covered overhead like a ceiling. Suddenly, Mother appeared at the back of the truck and shouted, "Ivy, you are going to ride up front to give more room to the others."

I cried, "No, no!"

Her brother, Uncle Bob, also pleaded, "Mary, please let her stay. There is plenty of room back here for all of us."

She screamed, "No!"

With the thought of being shut up with her and Daddy in the front seat of the truck, I took a chance by saying, "Why don't you take Susie?" Taking one look at our mother's face, I gave up the fight and crawled toward my worst nightmare.

As she pushed me up into the large shiny dump truck beside Daddy, she whispered, "You just want back there so you can tell all you know."

Sitting in between the two people who had stolen my childhood, I would not lean toward either one's shoulder to sleep. I sat straight up in the seat. Once on the road, Dad took my little hand and laid it over his pants' zipper. Mother had to see it when we passed lights, but she did nothing. I pretended to sleep all the time except when Daddy stopped for fuel. At those times, Uncle Bob and I unsuccessfully pleaded for Mother to let me have a turn in the back of the truck.

After an eight-hour trip, I awoke at daylight; and to my delight, Daddy had stopped the new dump truck in front of Granddad Ooking's building supply shop. This time, I did not run in to smell the King Edward cigar and Beech-Nut gum. I shied away from anyone who looked at me in order to stay out of any more trouble with Mother and Daddy.

There was still a housing shortage in our small hometown, so Granddad had rented us a house for the three summer months. I heard Mother say, "The Monroe family needs their house by the time school begins." Granddad had given the family in his apartment building next to the building supply shop notice to move, and we would move there when school began. Without furniture, Daddy and Uncle Bob placed wooden orange crates as our furniture in the living room, and Granddad purchased our bed frames for the mattresses, which were at the back of the dump truck.

After we were settled in our temporary home, Uncle Bob's ten-day furlough ended, and he had to meet his unit in California for a flight to Japan. When he picked up his duffel bag and began creeping toward the front door, the four of us children began screaming, "Do not leave us!"

Sadly, he replied, "You children make it hard for me to leave," as he grabbed his duffel bag and ran down the street.

With little furniture in the house to dust, I spent more time in the yard learning to play. My world looked beautiful, sitting in the green grass with a clear sky over me like a blue canopy. In addition, my brothers began including me in their game of hide-and-seek. Daddy would come out on the back porch, squat down, and lean against the post. In the excitement of getting to play, I ran fast to find a hiding place, and Dad would motion for me to come up on the porch. Frightened not to obey him, I came to him, and he covered me with the tarp that had been the ceiling of the dump truck. When his hands touched my body, I would scream; and immediately, he would lift the tarp and let me out. Of course, this always ended the game with my brothers singing, "Dumb Ivy is a troublemaker. You ruin all the fun."

The radios that hot July were tuned to the latest news concerning President Truman and the other world leaders at the Potsdam Conference trying to force the Japanese to surrender. Finally, Emperor Hirohito stated that Japan would accept the humiliation of an unconditional surrender.

During this time, Uncle Bob had been waiting in California to be transported to the war zone of Japan, and the family received the news that he would be home as soon as his orders were processed. By the time he arrived, we had moved from the Monroe house to the ugly wooden apartment building beside Granddaddy Ooking's building supply shop. At the end of the wooden overhead bridge stood a tall, thin, two-story building, which appeared to sway against the sky. The funny-looking building had a backdrop of lumber stacks from

Granddad's lumberyards. At the top of the tall building was our three-room apartment.

The first room would be a combination of our parents' bedroom and living room. The middle room had two full-size beds, one for Steve and the other one for Susie and me. Not only had Uncle Alfred, his wife, and little girl Sherry moved from the dairy farm to the other three-room apartment down the hall but they also had expanded their family with a new baby boy. Their family of four and our family of seven shared the one bathroom located midway down the L-shaped hall. At the end, the storage room had been cleared out so John and Uncle Bob had a bedroom.

On August 30, 1945, on my seventh birthday, I settled in to the sixth home since coming to live with this family four years earlier. For the first time, Mother mentioned "birthday cake" because Granddad Ooking would come to visit. She handed me a $1 bill and explained, "I would like to have an angel food cake for your birthday. Walk to the markets and buy one."

Reverting to the old confident child, I ran fast to show the green bill to my siblings. Everyone wanted to go to the store with me. Without my brothers, I could not have found the stores, so John led the way down the long stairway. We filed out the front door and turned right to begin our march down the street like ducks in a row. First, we passed Granddaddy's building supply shop. Then we crossed the intersection and stopped at the first market.

When we entered the little white building, the bell rang from above the door, which brought Mr. Reid from the back room. As he hobbled on his stiff leg using a cane, I kept looking in his face so he would not think that I had noticed his disability. I held up the bill and said, "I want to buy an angel food cake."

He smiled at the new kids on the block and answered, "I am sorry, but I do not have an angel food cake."

John opened the door, and we continued past the barbershop and drugstore and across the street. In the second block, we entered another small grocery store. I showed the man my dollar and proudly said, "It is my birthday, and I want to buy an angel food cake."

His reply made me feel special: "I do not have an angel food cake, but you are the first angel I have seen today!"

We marched back across the street in front of a big red brick schoolhouse surrounded by a large playground, and Steve informed me, "This is where we will start school next week."

All of us were disappointed that we could not find an angel food cake, and it never crossed our minds to buy another kind. I walked back up the steps and into the kitchen and handed Mother the dollar bill. She stood talking with Daddy. I had no idea they were talking about me. Suddenly, Daddy exploded, "Ivy, you better never walk out the street with all four of you together ever again. There is never to be more than two at any given time."

I dropped my head and answered, "Uh-hum."

He continued, speaking louder. "I was sitting in the barbershop when the four of you passed in a row. I never want to be embarrassed like that again."

With my head still down, watching to see if his hands went for his belt, I answered, "Uh-hum."

He came at me, gnashing his teeth, and I feared he would hit me with his hands. Instead, livid, he screamed even louder, "You answer me 'yes, sir'!"

I repeated, "Yes, sir."

Enraged, he continued. "Look me in the eye when you answer me." His flushed face brought memories of Baltimore flashing through my mind as I stood waiting for the belt. Agitated, he began again. "Say 'yes, sir,' and 'no, sir.'" He stormed. I repeated those phrases many times back to him as my siblings looked on, wide-eyed.

Infuriated, he demanded, "Look at your mother and say 'yes, Mama,' and 'no, Mama,' to her." I turned like a robot and looked at the woman who had a look as if she enjoyed tormenting a child in front of her children. I recited the words to Mother as she gave me one of those looks that turned my stomach in swirls of fear.

I heard Daddy shout again, "You better never forget that I do not want the four of you walking out on the street together." In a frenzy, he picked me up and threw me across the room, hitting the right side of my head on the metal springs of my bed. Mother and Daddy returned to the kitchen, and I crawled into bed and hid under the quilt.

Because of my anguished situation, I became quite excited to start school and to hear that Mother would be working as the bookkeeper at the building supply shop next door. However, this increased my chores because, when I returned from school, I had to take care of Susie—who stayed down the hall with Aunt Sue—and start dinner.

The principal at school suggested that, since our county did not rate students like Baltimore class assignments of A-1, A-2, B-1, and B-2, John, Steve, and I should be set back a year.

My teacher, Mrs. Calloway, had white hair and spoke softly like Mother's mother, Mama, and I felt confident in her class. One afternoon, she turned from writing on the blackboard to see a boy blow a large bubble with Bazooka bubble gum. The teacher used the boy as an example to anyone who might want to chew gum in class and demanded, "Spit that bubble gum in the wastebasket." Slowly, the sad little boy walked to the front of the room, opened his mouth, and dropped the large pink wad of gum into the overflowing wastebasket.

A piece of bubble gum was on the endangered species list, along with sugar and chocolate during the war years. The bright pink Bazooka sat high up on a white sheet of paper visible to all the first graders under the pencil sharpener. I saw other students picking up their pencils, and I jumped out of my seat and ran to the front to sharpen mine. As I turned to go back to my seat, I grabbed the gum. I had not planned on the gum being stuck to a full sheet of paper. This served as a flag to tell all the children that I had the gum. Many of the students began shouting, "Ivy took the bubble gum out of the trash can."

Mrs. Calloway replied, "No! She would not do such a thing."

Then the class ganged up on me, shouting, "Yes, she did."

I walked to the front and pretended to put the gum back in the can. Before I could return to my desk, the students again sang, "Teacher, Ivy did not do it!" Mrs. Calloway continued writing on the board and never mentioned it again.

Since the beginning of World War II, the only way to get certain items, such as chewing gum, was to know someone who owned a store, which I did not. I learned to walk the sidewalks and watch for gum. There were times when I sat and pulled the gum from the concrete. I just could not let a piece of gum get away from me!

My desire for sweets, soda, balloons, Shirley Temple movies, and bubble gum kept me in trouble. One morning I noticed that my friend

Patsy had left a quarter just inside her desk. Since she was my reading partner, I moved up to sit with her, and I took the money when the bell rang for recess. I invited Patsy to go downstairs and have a Pepsi and a bar of candy with me. We held our big tall Pepsi bottle for all to see while we ate a bar of candy, and I still had a nickel left. When the bell rang at the end of the day, Patsy began crying, "My quarter for a pair of socks is missing."

The teacher asked, "Class, did any one of you see Patsy's money?"

"No" was the response.

That afternoon, I felt horrible and guilty for upsetting my friend, so I hurried to Aunt Sue's apartment to get Susie. As usual, I wanted to take time to hold their new baby boy before I went home to peel potatoes. If Matt slept, I pinched his little fat leg. When he cried, I would ask, "Sue, will it be all right if I hold the baby since you are busy?" I learned—as usual, the hard way—that pleasures also had responsibilities. As I stood in the kitchen doorway talking to my aunt, I dropped the baby! Fortunately, he was not hurt, and I did as I had been instructed and took Susie to our apartment to peel potatoes.

Mother surprised me by arriving home from work early, and she came into the kitchen to tell me, "Your daddy wants to see you in the front room."

Immediately, I dropped the knife in the pot of potatoes and walked toward his bedroom. At the sight of his bright red face, I knew I was in trouble. He hit me with an element of surprise before he hit me with the belt. "Where did you get the money to buy Pepsi and candy at school?" I wondered how he knew. He repeated, "Where did you get the money you spent at school today?"

He began taking off his belt, and I lied, "Granddad gave it to me."

Daddy wrapped the belt around my legs as he screamed, "Where did you get the money you spent at school today?"

I cried, "I stole it from my friend."

He wrapped his belt around my body repeatedly before telling me to go get in my bed. I lay there unable to get my breath. *What would he do next?* He paced back and forth through my room to the kitchen and back to his room like a wild animal.

As was customary, the parents taught their children real object lessons through my behavior. However, unknown to the parents, what they really were doing was training their children how to misbehave successfully without getting caught like Dumb Ivy. Before the night ended, exasperated, Dad came to my bed, shouting, "Ivy, the principal best never have to call me again. Take this quarter to school tomorrow, give it to the girl, and you apologize to her."

The next morning, I handed Patsy the quarter and told her, "I am sorry for stealing your money."

She kindly replied, "Now I can buy a pair of socks."

The beatings and my wild screaming had distressed everyone in the apartment building. One evening Uncle Alfred shouted, "All children in my apartment, I have bubble gum!" The four of us ran over one another getting out the door and down the hall and joined their daughter, Sherry, in a circle on the floor.

Before the bubble-blowing contest began, we softened up our gum. I even popped a couple of large bubbles in my face, making everyone laugh. Just as the contest began, I looked up, and there stood Daddy at the door, motioning for me to come with him. I stopped laughing and began screaming, "No, no!"

My uncle pleaded, "Please, let Ivy stay and play with the others. She never gets to join the children."

Daddy replied, "No! She is a troublemaker."

When I entered our apartment, Mother walked up, stuck her finger in my mouth, took the gum, and told me to sit on the bed. I sat there listening to the children laughing and popping bubble gum as Dad began. He accused me of sexual behavior that I did not understand before lapping his belt around my body. My wild screams echoed through the hallways, which did not even draw the others' attention because it had become a regular part of life. Dad finally got in bed, and Mother dropped her dress to the floor. The noises they made frightened me. Quietly, I slid off the bed. Crawling on my belly to the next room, I got in my bed and covered my head with the quilts.

The next memorable lesson I learned was when I opened a package that did not have my name on it. After school, as I peeled potatoes, Susie brought a package in the kitchen that the mail carrier just left. Since our mail always went to Granddad's building supply shop, the only thing we knew to do with a package was to open it. Therefore, I took the potato knife and popped the string; and before our eyes, a beautiful pair of wedge-heel shoes shone back at us. Susie tried them on. They were excessively big, and I wore them around the kitchen—flop, flop—playing grown-up when our mother appeared in the doorway. Instantly, she became enraged when she saw her shoes on my feet. "How dare you open my package? If those shoes do not fit, I will not be able to send them back now that you have gotten them dirty."

Later, Dad came into the kitchen while I washed the dinner dishes to ask, "What name was printed on the package you opened?"

Looking him in the eye, I answered, "I do not know, sir."

As the children gathered around to see live violence before the era of television, he continued. "No one is to ever open a package unless their name is printed on the label, or they will be in big trouble."

I answered, "Yes, sir."

He looked me in the eye and asked, "Tell me why you put those shoes on when they did not belong to you."

I mumbled, "I wanted to see if they fit me."

Faster than I could blink an eye, he had the belt off and replied, "Well, let's just see if this fits you." I screamed and screamed as the belt kept wrapping around my body in the little cotton housedress.

Another way I lived on the edge was going to the grocery store for the next day's food supply after I finished the nightly dishes. Once Mr. Reid had bagged all the items on Mother's list, I paid him and went into my Hollywood act. With the brown grocery bag sitting on the ice cream cooler, I would press my finger against my cheek and, looking puzzled, say, "I know I have forgotten something. Let me think!"

The gentle Mr. Reid always smiled at me before saying, "While you try to remember, I will be in the back room."

As soon as the swinging door stopped moving, I had the cooler lid up and grabbed an ice cream, Brown Mule. I could still hear the little bell ringing as I ran out into the night. The chocolate coating fell from the vanilla ice cream as I tried to gulp it down and carry groceries. Since I could not eat all the ice cream off the stick before reaching the apartment, I threw it away. It never dawned on me to stand outside and finish eating before going upstairs.

However, the day Mother sent me to Crawford's Market ended my grocery store thievery. I entered the store. When I did not see anyone,

I leaned over to look at the candy bars. Just as I chose one and stuck it under my jacket, the owner said, "What do you have under your jacket?"

Scared to move, I replied, "My hand."

She demanded, "Turn around and let me see what you put under your jacket."

I became more fearful than embarrassed when I thought, *What if Daddy hears about this?* Quickly, I pulled my hand out from under my jacket, handed the candy bar to the angry woman, and ran from the store.

I heard those frightful words as she shouted, "If you ever steal again, I will call your granddaddy."

One positive aspect about Uncle Bob returning home from the war was that not only did he begin working at Granddaddy's store but he also took a great interest in me. First, he made me a deal. If I brushed my frizzy naturally curly hair at least one hundred times a day, he would pay me 10¢ a week. Second, I could earn another dime for every A that I received on my report card, and he would study with me.

Most evenings, when I finished the dishes, I ran to get the brush, and Uncle Bob used the occasion to have me count to one hundred as I brushed. After that, he reviewed my ten spelling words on the list for weekly tests. The first half of first grade, I made straight As.

Then in the excitement of the first holidays, I really understood what Santa Claus was all about; I ended up being Dumb Ivy again. One cold, snowy night, my two elder brothers led me across the wooden bridge to go see Santa in a furniture store. Our footsteps caused the boards to pop and crack on the bridge. Then my brothers stopped halfway and looked down at the train cars on the railroad tracks, and I cried, "Could we please get off this bridge? Mother says this bridge will fall one day."

Once on the west side, I saw my first Santa sitting in the window of a furniture store. I loved the happy laughing man at first sight and sat on his lap. Santa said, "What one item do you want me to bring you this year?"

I answered with a big smile, "A Mickey Mouse watch."

He replied, "Well, you better be a good girl."

When we entered the apartment, Mother asked the boys, "What did you tell Santa you wanted for Christmas?"

My brothers began laughing when they replied, "You won't believe that Dumb Ivy asked for a Mickey Mouse watch, and she can't even tell time." Mother's two brothers heard them laughing at me, and Uncle Bob and Uncle Clarence borrowed a large, school-size round clock. The two uncles spent hours teaching me the difficult concept of sixty seconds in a minute and sixty minutes in an hour.

I could not remember what I received that Christmas, but it wasn't a watch. Nevertheless, Uncle Bob, as usual, came to the rescue; and for Christmas, he introduced the family to music by giving us a 78 rpm record player. My favorite song was "The Old Lamplighter," and I memorized every word.

The long cold, snowy winter months faded and became alive with the blossoming of spring. Rows of yellow daffodils and multicolored tulips stood out on the blanket of bright green grass. The high, thick hedge that lined the front of the school lawn protected us from the fast-running vehicles on the street.

The tree branches that hung over the play area burst forth with buds. They also kept grass from growing on the permanent hopscotch imprinted in the ground. I loved recess because I had become one of the top five players in hopscotch, jacks, and jumping rope. I dreaded the last day of school, and I knew it would be the end of playing until I began second grade.

On my final report card, I had earned some dimes because I had made all As and Bs, with a perfect attendance certificate and a comment on my report card saying, "Ivy talks too much in class," which Mother used to prove how I caused trouble everywhere I went.

School dismissed for the summer. Our parents had secretly arranged to have mine and John's adenoids and tonsils removed. They knew the horrible fit I threw when I saw a police officer, a uniformed taxi driver, or an elevator operator ever since Dad raped me and took me to the hospital and the police came. Anytime I had to go to the doctor or dentist, they chased me around the room because I knew they would hurt me also.

One morning I thought it strange that the family was out of bed before Daddy left for work and that no one could have a drink of water.

Then fear set in when Mother took John and me downstairs, and we got in the car with Daddy. When we crossed the bridge, he parked on Main Street. I stayed close to John as we climbed the long staircase to the second floor. At the top, Daddy opened a door, and I saw a woman in a white dress. I began screaming, "No, no!"

The nurse put John in one of the twin beds and tried to get me in the other one. I would not go near it until I saw how sad my brother looked, so I joined him. However, when it was time to put the mask over my mouth, I tried to scream as my parents held me down to inhale the horrible-smelling ether, which soon floated me into peace.

The next thing I could remember was a woman's voice repeatedly calling, "Ivy." Again and again, I heard the nurse calling from way behind me. "Please come back." I kept floating farther and farther away from the voice, along with the clouds and over an ocean.

Periodically, I would cry out, "No! I am not coming back because they hurt me!"

Suddenly, my eyes opened to the pleading voice of the nurse, and she smiled and said, "You, young lady, gave us quite a scare."

She stepped aside, and to my horror, Mother stepped forward to say, "Look over there at your daddy. He has smoked two packs of cigarettes while waiting for you to wake up."

I heard my brother groan as he tried to swallow. He and I agreed this had to be the cruelest thing on earth for children; all the ice cream we wanted, and we could only chew aspirin gum for the sore throat.

When we recovered from the tonsillectomies, the nicest surprise since coming to live with this family was when all four children were enrolled in the summer program at the school's playground. For the first time since I was three years old, I felt good following the pretty teenage supervisor around the playground.

That summer, mainly when I played on the front steps of the school, periodically, I would hear my name lightly whispered up in the air. "Ivy." I stopped, looked, listened, and never saw anyone trying to get my attention. Each time, I decided not to answer; it had to be Mother calling from my granddaddy's store, diagonally across the street, for me to come home and do chores. If I had heard the Bible story of the boy Samuel, who heard his name being called, with Eli instructing him, "If you are called again, say, 'Speak, for your servant is listening,'" I would have known God wanted my attention.

Sitting on a swing at the playground, my neighborhood friend Patsy was the first person to tell me about Sunday school. She told me about the fun she had at the Kee Street Methodist Church, a couple of blocks behind the school. Since Granddad Ooking closed his business on Saturday afternoon, I learned that the next morning would be Sunday school. That first time, I got out of bed, dressed, and left the apartment while everyone slept.

The first time I walked into Sunday school, I felt safe and loved the people, and they were singing "Jesus Loves Me." The miracle of it all was that I was not afraid to say or sing the word *love* at church, which was considered a dirty word in our home.

I memorized the schedule of events as the pastor announced them on Sunday mornings because I did not want to miss anything. Miraculously, if my chores were done, Mother let me go to church anytime. I adopted the church people as my family and Jesus, who loved me. There was also Ms. Johnson, who gave me chewing gum. I did not realize that, after Sunday school, I could have sat with the girls from my class in church. Instead, I sat about five rows from the front to watch Ms. Johnson play the piano as my real mother had played for me.

One Sunday morning, after Ms. Johnson finished playing the hymns, the pastor began his sermon. The beautiful young woman turned and motioned for me to come to the front row with her. Slowly, I made my way down the aisle, only hesitating a second before sitting beside her, and oh, how good she did smell. I looked at her shiny black hair and sparkly black eyes. She wore red lipstick and matching nail polish.

For the next year, I sat waiting for her to motion for me to come up front after she finished playing the hymns. Every time she opened her pocketbook, she gave me a stick of chewing gum and put her arm around my shoulders until it was time for her to play the closing hymn.

The amazing thing was that I had the confidence to get out of bed on Sunday morning, tiptoe around to get dressed, and leave everyone in bed, that is, unless I could get Susie to go with me. Since I was not aware of time, I would walk in at the middle of Sunday school; or other times, church was already in progress.

The adults in the congregation loved me even when I did the most ridiculous things. I did not realize, when I heard the announcement of Wednesday night choir practice, that it was for high school through adult ages. I was the only child in the choir the summer I turned eight years old! I sat there on Wednesday nights, week after week, in the choir loft, not realizing that they were practicing for Sunday service. I never went up to the choir loft to sing with them for the worship services.

Whenever I was at church, I watched the activities around me as if I were sitting in a movie theater. At first, I feared that the high school couple Polly and Sonny, holding hands in front of their mothers, would get in trouble until one day I stood nearby as Sonny asked his mother for $2 to take Polly to a movie and have a hamburger. When she smiled and gave the money to him, it was the turning point when I knew boy-and-girl relationships were good. Of course, I had to keep it a secret that I began dreaming of the day that I would date.

Just before school started, one Saturday night, to my horror, Mother cut my long hair so short that I could not even twist it around my finger. I felt too ugly for the beautiful Ms. Johnson to see me, but rather than miss being with her, I pinned a scarf on my head with seven bobby pins on each side to make sure the scarf did not slide off. Neither the Sunday school teachers nor the students could talk me into telling them why I had the scarf pinned to my head.

Once Ms. Johnson motioned for me, she whispered, "Why are you wearing a scarf?"

Tears poured down my cheeks as I whispered back, "Mother cut my hair too short."

"I think you would look pretty with short hair," she whispered as she began pulling pins from one side while I pulled from the other. "Oh, how pretty you look." She handed me a stick of gum, and I leaned back on her arm.

I could not remember my eighth birthday. However, I did remember the first day of school. I took Susie to the line of my first-grade teacher's class from last year and tried to leave her so I could get in Mrs. James's second-grade line. Susie began to cry, "I want my mother."

The sad look on her face, the tears pouring from her, and the screams "I want my mother!" caused me to cry. I told Susie how much fun she would have with my last year's teacher, but when I turned to go, she continued screaming.

Finally, the teacher walked over to Susie and said, "What is wrong here?"

Susie screamed, "I want Mother!"

I began crying when the gentle teacher gave my sister a little spank on her behind and said, "You are going to stay in your line. And, Ivy, you go get in your line." I felt better at recess when I saw my sister running wild on the playground with her classmates.

My friendly second-grade teacher, Mrs. James, had a large smile and was soft-spoken. I did love learning reading, writing, and arithmetic. It was also the beginning of my social life. Joanne became my best friend mainly because she tap-danced like Shirley Temple.

Every Friday afternoon, everyone who could pay the 9¢ admission attended a movie in the school auditorium. If it happened to be a Shirley Temple movie, I begged, borrowed, and stole to get admission.

Every chance I got, I asked Joanne to go into the cloakroom and teach me to dance and sing like Shirley Temple. The day Joanne brought a record player to perform before the class, I could not believe it when she began dancing to my favorite record, "The Old Lamplighter." When we were not dancing and singing, we were sitting at the table with our first boyfriends. Oh, how I liked Donald, who bought me a tall bottle of Pepsi most days.

One afternoon, while the class practiced for the school play, when the music stopped, the teacher told the partners to drop hands. Donald and I kept holding hands. The teacher embarrassed us by saying, "Ivy and Donald, let go of your hands."

And the class began saying, "Shame on Ivy and Donald."

Every day at lunch, my brothers, Susie, and I walked a block home for pinto beans, potatoes, and corn bread. One night, I asked Mother if I could take a brown lunch bag to school. Since I had become a social animal, I needed to spend the lunch hour free to talk with my friends without getting in trouble with the teacher.

One day it was snowing; and as the snow became deeper, I pleaded with Mother, "Please let me go to the store and get something to pack in my lunch tomorrow."

I did not understand why she laughed at me until later when I heard her explain it to my brothers. "Dumb Ivy wants to walk past the school to the store and buy something to carry in her lunch."

Sure enough, the next morning, there was winter wonderland, and even the dirty old wooden bridge was white as snow. Susie and I wiggled into our snowsuits, and I pulled on my tight galoshes. At the bottom of the stairs, we paused before lifting our padded legs out into the snow and laughed as we sank up to our knees, trying to jump in the prints Daddy had left earlier. The snow stopped by lunchtime, and Susie and I literally screamed for joy as we walked through the deep drifts in the winter wonderland.

After lunch, we stood in the doorway of the apartment building. Instantly, we both became overwhelmed by the beauty of the moment. We dived into the snow and began rolling and laughing. For a second, we were the only two people in the world until I heard Daddy's voice. "You two get upstairs and get in bed!"

My joy turned to pleading. "Please don't make me miss school, or I won't receive a perfect attendance certificate."

"You should have thought of that before you rolled in the snow!" he snapped.

Since Granddad Ooking had hired a new bookkeeper, Mother now stayed home. Dad led us back up the steps and told Mother, "These girls are to stay in my bed until I get home from work, and then I will whip them."

Mother spent most of the afternoon in the kitchen listening to soap operas on the radio, leaving Susie and me to console each other in her bedroom. The long afternoon took its toll on my little sister's nerves, and she whispered to me, "What's it feel like to be whipped with Daddy's belt?"

The only way I could think of was to show her by pinching her arm and say, "Maybe something like this."

She would cry, "Oh, I am so scared!"

Off and on during the afternoon, she asked me to pinch her arm so she would be used to the pain before the whipping. I assured her, "After all these years, I have never gotten used to the belt."

However, it pleased me to have a real, live, warm person to help take the pressure off a long afternoon, which would end with the belt.

I felt ashamed to face Uncle Bob when he entered the front room with Dad after work. Every time my uncle saw me, I was in trouble, and he never gave up on me.

Just before the men finished their dinner, the unfairness of my position in the family hit rock bottom. Mother came in the bedroom and pulled Susie from the bed, and as they walked toward the kitchen, I heard Mother say, "See what happens to you when you play with Dumb Ivy?"

I hid my face when Bob walked past me on his way down the hall to his room. Dad entered the room carrying his belt, swishing toward my body, as I heard Mother say to Susie, "Go in the kitchen. I fixed your favorite hominy for dinner."

After the spanking, Mother told Daddy, "Let Ivy out of the bed so she can do the dishes."

Bob came back into the kitchen, and to break the silence, he teased, "Did you see the new refrigerator?"

I looked around the small room, smiled at him, and said, "No."

"Sure." As he opened the window, letting the snowy, cold air into the kitchen, he said, "I've shown it to all the other children. Here have a look." I looked out the window and began laughing when I saw that my uncle had nailed a shelf to the outside edge of the window, and there, high above the snowy ground, sat butter and buttermilk.

That same week, bigger and uglier situations arose, which I could have never anticipated. My brown snowsuit was too tight, and I had to struggle to pull up the trousers. I got in a hurry in the cloakroom, jerked the pants up too hard, and heard a rip but ignored it. When we got home, my brothers refused to miss their radio programs to go to the grocery store. Mother told me, "There is no need to take off your snowsuit until you go to the store."

I slumped on the couch in her bedroom, waiting until she completed the list. When she began staring, I jumped to a sitting position, and she asked, "How did you tear the crotch of your snow pants?"

The years of brainwashing had created in me the thought that any body part below my neck was dirty. I was even afraid to put my hands under the covers for fear that my parents would think I was touching my body. The tone of her voice caused a cold chill to run through me. I tried hard to explain the simple fact that I just pulled too hard, trying to get them on, and it tore. She promised, "Just wait until your daddy gets home."

After dinner, she sent my brothers and Susie to Uncle Alfred's apartment to play. She quipped, "After you finish the dishes, show Daddy your snow pants."

I stood as far away as I could when I said, "Mother wants you to see my snow pants."

Daddy replied, "What boy tore your snow pants?"

I stood confused, crying and watching the belt, when he asked a strange question: "Did a boy put his finger in the hole of your snowsuit?"

I sobbed, "No!" I wondered why a boy would want to do such a silly thing. While I was thinking, he put his belt in his hand and told me to sit on the bed. "Please do not make me sit on the bed!"

Before I had time to sit, the belt struck repeatedly, and Mother dropped her housedress to the floor. I scooted to the floor and covered my eyes and ears, and Mother kept repeating, "Ivy, stand up and look at us and stop that crying."

As winter in the mountains turned to a brilliant, colorful spring, I lost some of my protection when the children were outside playing. One evening Daddy called me to his bed. The large man with a fat stomach smiled at me like the big bully Junior, whom we were all afraid of at school. He confused me when he asked the strangest question: "Have you and Sherry been lying on Aunt Sue's bed with your hands in each other's panties?"

I looked at him quizzically and replied, "No!" To my delight, he let me go play with the children.

After my chores were finished the next night, he allowed me to go down the hall to Uncle Alfred's apartment. Sherry had just turned six, and I was about to complete second grade and turn nine in the summer. I remembered the suggestion that Daddy had made the night before. I said to my cousin, "I know what! Come over here and lie beside me on the bed, and we will put our hands in each other's pants."

Once we finished all the arrangements, I became bored lying there with our hands on each other's stomach. Just as I said, "I wonder why Daddy suggested such a crazy game," I looked up, and there he stood in the second doorway of my aunt's apartment.

He snapped, "You come home right this minute."

When I walked in our apartment, Daddy demanded, "Sit on the bed." He embarrassed me when he repeatedly described the scene to Mother. I could not understand why he had gotten so angry when he had been the one who suggested the game. After whipping me, he let the belt fall to the floor, and Mother dropped her housedress.

The majority of the time, Daddy stretched the whippings out between cross-examinations. The sessions would last anywhere from one to many hours. While enduring the sessions, helplessly, I watched Mother stand guard at the door and thought how much more I hated her than Daddy. At those moments, I wished everyone could see her because of the many times I had sat listening to her tell others that she put up with an unfaithful husband, kept her Bible by the bedside, did not drink, and washed and ironed and kept the house clean.

Whenever I got home from school, Mother assigned me to iron everything except the starched items, dust and mop the floors, and assist her in the kitchen while her children went out to play. To cover the fact that I did most of her chores, Mother made sure that I had the ironing board and dust mop put away and the table set for dinner before Daddy and Bob arrived. Then they would see me sitting idly on my bed, waiting to wash dishes so I could run off to church.

One Wednesday evening, I pleaded, "If the boys do not hurry and finish eating their dinner, I will not have the dishes finished in time to go practice the Easter music." I began begging Susie. "Please hurry and finish your dinner."

Just then, we heard the man who collected our uncle's leftovers for his pigs coming up the steps to transfer the slop from the hall container into his bucket. Twice a week, this large older man in bib overalls arrived at the top of the steps, saying, "Got any scraps today?"

One day when Susie heard him, she quickly handed me her plate and left the room. As I stood at the sink, a loud "ouch!" flowed through the apartment. I ran behind Steve to the hall to see Susie standing there with a sewing needle in her hand. She had heard someone tease, "When the old man leans over to empty the containers, his behind would make a good target." After that, the man would not collect if anyone stood in the hall. It confused me why my brothers and sister never got in trouble for the pranks they played, yet I got into serious trouble for things I had not even done.

That same spring, I returned home from choir practice, and Mother began a new accusation with my brothers. At least I was glad Dad wasn't home with the belt. However, the frustration of trying to defend myself in front of my siblings made my nose bleed as Mother falsely reported, "Dumb Ivy has not been to church, and she has been lying with boys on the school playground."

The first time, I screamed and cried, "Yes, I did go to church. Yes, I did." I could not understand why she thought I would lie on the playground and get my clothes dirty.

The fresh spring air made me feel light and lively as Susie and I walked to church on Easter Sunday. Granddad Ooking gave Mother the money to order Easter outfits from the Sears, Roebuck & Co. catalog. My dress had beautiful large yellow sunflowers on it. Best of all, Ms. Johnson invited my sister to sit with us, and she gave both of us a stick of gum.

That same spring, I wore my sunflower dress to church on Mother's Day, and I bribed Susie into going with me by saying, "You know Ms. Johnson will give you a stick of gum."

For the first time when we arrived back at the apartment, there was no one in the building. This frightened us, and Susie began crying, "I want my mother."

I remembered the pastor making an announcement about something going on at the church at one o'clock. I told her, "Do not cry. We are going back to church."

We walked up the church steps, and there stood strangers in black suits. When we entered the church, nothing looked normal as people filed down the aisle and looked in a box. I took my little sister by the hand, led her down to the front of the church, and lifted her to see the beautiful woman inside the coffin. She had on a pink dress with a cameo pin on the white collar, white hair, and a peaceful smile of her face. Susie asked in a loud voice, "When will she wake up?"

I answered, "I've never been to a church service like this."

When we arrived back at the apartment, Mother bragged, "While you were at church, the family took flowers to Grandmother for

Mother's Day." Mother knew I would cry when she told me she had been to see Granddad Ooking.

"Let's look in the paper and see whose funeral Dumb Ivy took Susie to." I heard her tell the boys, "Can you believe it? They went to the funeral of Pastor Yost's wife!"

I begged to wear my new Easter sunflower dress to the last day of second grade because all the girls were going to dress up. The teacher gave out report cards, and when I saw the half day marked under Absent, I realized that the roll in the snow had cost me a perfect attendance certificate. Sadly, I walked toward the apartment, and Uncle Bob came out of the building supply shop and paid me a dime for every A and a nickel for every B on my report card. He made another deal with me for the summer months: "Now that school is out, I will pay you 10¢ for every pair of my shoes you polish."

When Mother had assigned my summer chores, she sent her children out to play in Granddad Ooking's lumberyard. Whenever I went to Bible school, choir practice, or any church function, Mother called her children in the house to be with her.

I did not know why Mother asked me to do a strange thing the next morning—"Wrap all the dishes in newspapers and put them in a box"—until John came to carry the boxes downstairs. He explained, "Dad rented a house in the country just for the summer."

Upon hearing this, I began screaming, "I do not want to leave my church!" Not being conscious of it at the time, the adults who cared for me at church, the singing of "Jesus Loves Me," and Ms. Johnson's kindness to me had given me an inner strength to withstand the horrible abuse at home.

My brother helped calm my fears when he continued. "We will only live in the country three months until a house near the school and your church will be available."

When we arrived at the little, two-bedroom white-framed house, which sat on a rocky country road one mile from the nearest neighbor, I panicked because I needed the security of being around people. This house seemed more like a hundred miles from the city limits instead of five. Besides the two bedrooms, there was a living room, dining room, kitchen, and a small room, which would eventually be the bathroom.

Susie and I claimed that room for our first private bedroom. We were very proud that we had a skeleton key to lock the door.

We did not have inside running water, and we were to use our first outhouse. Daddy and Uncle Bob hauled a five-hundred-gallon barrel of water to the side yard and connected it to the kitchen sink with conduit.

After the men left for work in the mornings, I helped with the washing, hanging out clothes, dust mopping, and ironing. After I set the table for the two men's lunch of pinto beans, potatoes, and corn bread, Mother then allowed me to play outside if I promised to leave her children alone.

It was not long after we moved that the boys came running into the kitchen one Sunday morning with alarming news. "Uncle Bob did not sleep in his bed last night." There were cries of fear throughout most of the day as the four of us children waited for our uncle.

Late in the evening, Mother came out on the front porch, saying, "If my brother does not sleep in his bed tonight, Daddy will notify the police that he is missing." She looked at her boys and continued. "You boys are missing your Sunday night radio shows."

The four of us went in and lay on the floor in front of the radio until it was time to go to bed. There were four little noses sniffling until Mother came in the hallway to announce, "Bob just came home. Daddy is out in the yard talking to him, and no one is to ask Bob any questions about where he has been." A great loud shout arose from the two bedrooms of grieving children. That was the beginning of his mysterious disappearances every weekend.

All the problems that I feared might happen by living in an isolated area came true during the long weekends of unbearable summer heat. Daddy would find reasons to whip me or hold me down on the bed and tickle me until I passed out from screaming.

The evenings when Uncle Bob was home, I had to sit in a chair in the corner of my parents' bedroom. I would lay my head over on the Singer sewing machine and listen to the faint voices of my brothers and Susie playing outside. The children would ride the scooter, the kiddie car, and the little red wagon bumpily up the road and gag at the dust as they accelerated the toys.

We did not have a telephone or visitors to interrupt the violent and exhausting times I spent in my parents' bedroom on weekends. As Daddy popped questions that I could have never answered, Mother stood guard at the door. I learned to take comfort in the songs that I had learned in church and would sing them in my mind. I could especially find peace when I thought of the words to "What a Friend We Have in Jesus" and "Jesus Loves Me." ("This I know because the Bible tells me so.")

Late one Saturday afternoon, after spending most of the day in their room, Susie tried to hide me by taking the skeleton key to our small bedroom and locking us in the room. We sat in the corner under a pile of clothing when I heard the call "Ivy, come here."

Frightened, I tried the key, and the door would not open. Finally, our parents were standing outside our room, shouting, "Open this door this minute."

Susie and I cried together, "We cannot get the key to unlock the door!"

Daddy demanded, "Slide the key under the door."

He unlocked the door and took me to his room as I listened to Mother tell Susie, "I have told you to stay away from that troublemaker, Dumb Ivy."

One evening while I was washing dishes, I saw Granddad Ooking drive into the yard in a brand-new car. From the kitchen window, I watched Granddaddy talking with my siblings, and I knew he would give them a stick of Beech-Nut gum. Hastily, I swished the dish towel through the bean pot and pulled out a towel covered with brown juice. In my panic, I hid it.

The next morning, Mother scolded, "I found the dish towel you hid and have a mind not to tell you what Granddaddy Ooking has planned for you."

I cried, "I will never do it again. Please tell me."

She continued. "Beginning Monday morning, you will start Bible school back at Kee Street Church."

I jumped up and down, asking how I would get there, and Mother continued. "You will ride to work with Daddy and Uncle Bob and stay at the lumber supply shop until it was time to walk on to church."

Rising early Monday morning, I dressed in a cotton dress with a sash torn from one side and happily climbed into the large truck between Daddy and my uncle. When I stood in front of the store, I soaked in all the familiar sights of the apartment building, school playground, and the little grocery stores.

I felt important when I walked into the building supply shop. Immediately, the telephone caught my attention. I was almost nine years old, and I had never talked on a telephone. I could not understand why, every time I picked up the receiver, a woman would say, "May I help you?"

I would put the receiver back in the cradle and try again, and every time, I would hear, "May I help you?"

Suddenly, the telephone rang, and I heard the bookkeeper say, "Operator, I assure no one will be playing with the telephone again." There was something comfortable about that scene of a bookkeeper writing in ledgers and of coffee cups and a telephone on the tables. I decided at that moment that I would be a bookkeeper someday.

In the meantime, I continued my first real tour of the building supply business. I ran to kegs of big, small, fat, skinny, and dirty nails. Since my job at home had always been to keep everything clean, I began wiping the nails and got my hands covered in grease. When my granddaddy told me to wash up and leave for Bible school, I decided I did not want to clean my hands. I did not take the shortcut through the school playground to church. Instead, I walked down the street swinging my hands for all to see that I had been working.

On one of those mornings, a woman from the neighborhood stopped to inquire, "Ivy, what is on your hands?"

I gave her a frown to show I had been working before saying, "Oh, I am so tired from working at my granddaddy's store."

She smiled, patted me on the head, and said, "What a cute girl."

Granddaddy had not been happy with my torn dress when I arrived the first day, and he gave Mother the money to buy me new church clothes. I had never seen Mother sew on her Singer sewing machine! However, to please her money source, two days later, I arrived at the store for Granddad to see me in a homemade dress, which was called a pinafore instead of a dress.

After two relaxing, fun weeks at Bible school, parents and teachers took all the children to the park for a picnic. I sat in the backseat of a woman's car by a large brown bag, which I knew was full of food. When we arrived at the park, no one could coax me out of the car. Finally, one of the teachers said, "Everyone leave her alone and go play."

When I saw they were all busy, I slipped my hand into the full grocery bag and fished out a package of cold wieners. I had never seen one before. The first one tasted great, the second one okay, and the third one made me feel sick to my stomach. So I got out of the car and went to sit on the grass and watch the children run and chase one another. When the wieners were roasted, the teachers knew why I could not eat one thing!

However, I came alive on Sunday morning when the Bible school classes were to present a program for our parents. Rising early, I dressed myself in the sunflower dress and black and white saddle oxfords and waited for Daddy to drive me to church. Only Mother appeared and snapped, "How dare you disturb the family on the only day we have to sleep late?" Then she dropped a bombshell. "You are not going to church today. Daddy is too tired."

Because of the abuse I had endured, I had become withdrawn and shy and had never spoken out, much less voiced an opinion. In a few weeks, I would be nine years old, two and a half years older than Susie. Many times, Mother had told me, "Susie has the beauty of Daddy's sister and the intelligence to go with it." Whenever Susie voiced her opinions, all eyes were on her, including mine and those of my brothers.

Somehow, at that important moment in my life, I drew strength from my sister's outspokenness. I began screaming, "I have to go to church. I have a part in the play."

Then suddenly, I knew that I would sit in their bedroom all day when I heard Daddy call Mother back into the bedroom. Instead, she returned and walked to the boys' room, and I heard her tell John, "Daddy wants you to walk Ivy to the church. The fastest way to get her there on time is to take the shortcut along the railroad tracks."

I was pleasantly surprised at how patient and considerate my eldest brother was in taking this journey as he led me behind the outhouse and down over the hill to the railroad tracks. He helped me up on the tracks, and I followed him. I got lost in the moment of walking the tracks and forgot about being on time for the Bible school program. When I did become conscious of my mission, I looked up, and we were under the wooden overhead bridge.

When we left the tracks, crossed the creek, and began walking on the sidewalk in front of Granddad's store, I saw the mud on my saddle oxfords. I began crying, "I cannot go to church with mud on my shoes."

John asked me, "Why don't you go in the drugstore and wash your shoes off in the bathroom?"

After I had wiped them with wet toilet paper, John grabbed my hand and began running toward the church. He prepared me that I would be late. At the top of the steps, I heard my friends singing my favorite song, "Jesus Loves Me."

As I walked down the aisle to find my seat, tears began to roll down my cheeks when I noticed that I had only smeared the mud over my shoes with the wet toilet paper. I picked up, singing the verse, "For I am weak, but he is strong. Yes, Jesus loves me."

The month before we moved back to town, our mother surprised us by directing a nature walk. She pointed out the names of plants and insects. This wasn't like the woman I knew, especially when she picked a flower from the dogwood tree and began, "It's in the shape of the cross that Jesus hung on, and the red stains represent his shed blood."

With the long hot summer ending, one afternoon, Mother placed a laundry tub on the high back porch. As if standing at a very tall pulpit, she announced to the four of us below, looking up at her, "Before we move, I am going to scrub everyone in my washtub."

I became paralyzed with fear. Many nights in years gone by, from my bed, I could hear Mother giving my siblings baths in the kitchen. But never me! Now that she was giving everyone a bath in the tub, I became petrified at the thought of her seeing my black belly.

While she bathed the others, I went in the outhouse and tried to roll dirt from my stomach. When I saw the red skin from where I had rubbed so hard, I became frightened that Mother would accuse me of something. I didn't know of what, but it would be something bad.

Sitting on a large rock in the yard, I watched as the last sibling stepped out of the tub and Mother wrapped her in a towel. I panicked, as it was my turn. However, Mother tilted the tub, poured the bathwater over the side, and took the children inside for a treat. Stunned, I sat on the big old rock until dark and did not know whether to shout for joy or cry from rejection.

The next day, Bob and Daddy began putting the furniture on the dump truck again. I asked John, "Where are we moving this time?"

His answer pleased me very much when he reported, "We are moving five blocks from school and your church."

By my ninth birthday, the summer of 1947, we arrived at our small two-bedroom stucco house, which was the last in a block of clustered little white-framed homes. I hurried into the house to find Bob and my brothers moving two full-size beds for them into the largest bedroom off the living room. Susie and I were going to bunk in the living room on a folding cot. An archway separated the living room and dining room. Once in the dining room, a turn to the left took you straight into Daddy and Mother's bedroom. Straight ahead was the bathroom and right to go into the kitchen.

Somehow, when I spied out my parents' bedroom, I was not surprised to find privacy by their side of the house. They had a one-hundred-foot-wide field, which sloped downward to another one hundred feet in length. Out of the kitchen, I stood high up on the back porch where the long downward-sloping backyard went straight up another hill for a couple of blocks to the nearest neighbor.

When time came to begin third grade, I looked forward to going back to the big brick school building across from Granddaddy's building supply shop. It was not to be. I learned that I would be going to an annex building only two doors up from my church. I screamed and cried.

The annex was a large, two-story old house, which consisted of only four classes—third- and fourth-grade classes upstairs and a third and fourth downstairs. Three blocks from my house, I turned left on Capes Street and entered the country-style house. Through the first door on the right on the first floor, I entered the third-grade classroom. To make matters worse, my teacher, Ms. White, had a reputation of being a serious, strict teacher, which was true.

Within the week, I did not understand what had happened when the girls gathered around me to be their leader. The boys had to stay on the right side of the schoolhouse, while the girls played on the left side of the building. As if it had always been my position to be leader, both third-grade classes automatically flocked around me, and the girls argued over whose turn it was to hold my hand.

They also bombarded me with requests, such as "Can we play farmer in the dell? May I be the farmer!" "Why not ring-around-the-rosy?" "I want to play drop the handkerchief." "What are we going to play?" When the questions began to fly, it seemed natural for me to take charge here with these girls when I withdrew everywhere else.

Between my school and church, there were a few trees and a couple of houses. However, when I began third grade in the annex, I lived in such a small world that, most of the time, I did not know that my church was in shouting distance of the school. When I asked my family how to get to church, they had a hoot: "Poor Dumb Ivy."

At church, unlike school, no one had heard me speak more than fifty words. I just sat and watched the people I loved being around with. After three months of absence, how wonderful and comfortable it was to be back, and beautiful Ms. Johnson motioned for me to come and sit with her again.

The greatest shock in my absence of three months was when Mother's childhood pastor became the new pastor at Kee Street. I immediately liked him because he had features and a personality that reminded me of Granddaddy Ooking. Because I had a birthday while away, I had become old enough to attend the Sunday school class of two women (teenagers) whom I had grown to love—Jean and Dean, the twin sisters.

Pastor Donnelly paid a visit to Mother. She occasionally attended Wednesday night prayer meeting with me just to please her former pastor. Standing beside her made me feel proud to have family in the church. Mainly, I found it hard to believe that she knew the hymns that I had grown to love. I did not understand it, but when she attended, I felt more a part of the people in the congregation.

Another great person came into my life when I returned to church—the pastor's wife, who had a beautiful smile and snow-white hair and who spoke softly. Whenever her granddaughter, Mona, visited for the weekend, Mrs. Donnelly invited me to the parsonage, and it had to be like going to heaven for a child. I played without fear of upsetting anyone and being locked in a bedroom for the day. The stage was set for my third-grade year at church and school; I was to suffer the worst year of my life.

Once it started, it was like a freight train, and there was no stopping the momentum. First, one lunchtime, after washing the dishes, I ran to school so as not to be late. On the way, I found a balloon. When I entered the classroom, as I was letting the air out, simultaneously, the tardy bell rang, and Junior stuck a pin in the balloon. *Pop!* The teacher instructed, "Ivy, do you know the rule that anyone playing with a balloon after the bell rings gets a paddling?" I could still see the looks on my friends' faces as their leader leaned over the front desk and got three licks by the teacher.

Believe me, that was one long, cold, snowy, and painful winter. Ms. White gave us plenty of time on snowy days to put on our snow gear before going outside. She chose the first row that had sat up straight, feet on the floor and hands on desks, to go first to the coat closet. One snowy afternoon, my row went in first, and the metal coat hanger the teacher hung her coat on had fallen to the floor. Just as I got to the exit door, I slid on the hanger and, to keep from falling, caught myself while facing the door. Just as I realized that I had avoided the fall, I heard Ms. White say, "Ivy, you know the rule. Anyone caught skating in the cloakroom gets a paddling!"

The trauma of being paddled twice by Ms. White soon passed as she restored my leadership by asking me to go to the store or take a note to the teachers on the second floor for her. Whenever she sent me upstairs, I hated to enter the fourth-grade class where Donald threw kisses and winked at me. He caused me to panic when he would shout every time he saw me, "One of these days, I will kiss Ivy."

Then there was my best girlfriend, a tomboy, who lived one street over but her backyard facing straight across the street from our front door. One day Shirley and her sister Amy were sitting on the back fence, shouting, "Ivy, come out and play with us," which never moved Mother to let me out to play after school.

One afternoon, I walked to the side of the house where the trash cans sat under my parents' bedroom window. Shirley jumped off the fence, ran to me, and said, "My sister says you are her girlfriend and wants to kiss you."

Fear! Mother was lying in bed. What if she heard that remark about kissing? And kissing a girl? I remember once hearing Susie singing, "John loves Jerry."

And Mother told her, "Boys have girlfriends, and girls have boyfriends."

I ran around the house through the back door and began dust mopping the floor harder than ever before. Mother only shouted, "You better get in this house and get busy!"

A few days later, I took the trash to the barrel in a torn old housedress. To my horror, the sisters were sitting on the fence. Just as I dropped the trash in the barrel and turned to leave, they began singing, "Ivy has a lazy mother who makes her do all the work."

Mother came out of her bed and demanded, "Dumb Ivy, get in the house, and I forbid you to associate with those sisters."

When winter arrived, I had a tragic experience as Shirley and I trudged home from school in a wintry blizzard. The conditions were so bad that we walked slowly on the sidewalk through deep, fresh snow with no tracks to step in. Donald and his friends were walking down the middle of the road in the tracks a couple of cars had made. Donald shouted, "I will kiss Ivy if someone will hold her down for me."

The third time he shouted, my athletic friend, with pigtails sticking out from under her cap, shouted back, "If you promise to kiss her, I can hold her."

By the time Donald waded across the snowdrifts in the drainage ditch between the road and the sidewalk, Shirley had my body pinned to a snowbank. Donald leaned over me, with his friends looking over his shoulder, and gave me a big kiss right in the mouth before they took off, pushing one another down in the snow. By now, the upper classes from the big brick building were close behind, and I heard one of the girls shout, "Donald just kissed your sister in the mouth!"

I did not care if I fell. I had to beat my brothers home. I had begun dust mopping the floors as hard and fast as I could when John and Steve entered the house. I felt the blood drain from my face when I heard them say, "Dumb Ivy was lying in the snow kissing a boy."

Mother replied, "Nothing Dumb Ivy does surprise me. Just wait until Daddy gets home."

For the first time since Daddy had given me the idea of playing the game with my cousin, he called me into his bedroom without my mother. This situation frightened me more because I had become accustomed to how he and Mother operated, and now I did not know what to expect.

However, when I shut the door behind me, he never once mentioned the boy's kiss, and he stunned me when he began, "What does —— spell?"

I thought of all the spellings and words Uncle Bob had taught me, and I had never heard that one. I replied, "I do not know that one, sir."

As he began taking off his belt, he repeated, "What does —— spell?"

I began to scream, "I do not know!" as he slapped the belt around my body in the thin cotton housedress. When he finished, he went out, sat down at the table for his dinner, and demanded, "Ivy, bring me a glass of water."

The next day, my eyes were swollen from crying, and I was weak from the whippings; I had a worse ordeal. As Shirley and I walked home from school, she stopped to talk with a friend, knowing that Mother only gave me ten minutes from the time school let out to get in the house. I said, "Shirley, I have to get home."

She replied, "Wait, I want to walk with you."

Finally, knowing I was already late, I shouted, "Come on and quit your ——," and I spelled the word my dad had spelled to me the night before.

They began shouting, "Aaaaaaah, did you hear the word Ivy spelled?" By their overwhelming reaction, I knew it had to be a dirty word, and panic caused me to take off running for my life. I did something that I had never done without Mother's permission—I ran into a neighbor's house.

Gladys, a happy woman, welcomed me with open arms. There were times when Mother sent me to try on a dress Gladys was making for me. I loved going into her sewing room on the sunporch. I knew this family liked me because of the day Mother planned to take me for a bus ride to a nearby town to have my eyes examined. Gladys's kind and loving father handed me a $1 bill and said, "Buy yourself a gift."

I ran home waving the green dollar bill, shouting, "Mother, look what I have."

She took the bill from me, and that evening, when I finished the dishes, my parents called me into the bedroom. Mother took her place at the door while Daddy began the cross-examination. Repeatedly, he asked, "Tell me why you lay in the garden with Gladys's father for a dollar."

Desperately, I cried, "No, I didn't."

Now frantically running for my life, I ran into Gladys's house. She did not ask any questions, just poured a glass of milk and handed me a cookie. Before I could finish gulping down the refreshments, I heard John shouting as he came in her front door, "Ivy, Mother says to come home immediately."

I entered the front door with my head down, and Mother demanded, "Go into the bedroom and wait for Daddy."

For the second night in a row, Daddy came into his room before having pinto beans, potatoes, and corn bread. Not only did he leave the door ajar but he also shouted loudly enough for the family to hear, "No one in this family is going to use foul language. Do you understand me?" *Wham, wham!* And my nose began to bleed. Dad went to the door to ask Mother to bring a cold washcloth to hold on my nose so he could eat his dinner.

Afterward, Mother took her place at the door, Dad told me to sit up, and blood gushed forward from my nose. Mother told Dad, "Tear a piece off that brown bag and put it under her top lip. It will stop the bleeding."

When I had the paper in place, Mother instructed Daddy, "Go ahead continue. She will be all right."

Under normal circumstances, Mother and Daddy would be in their bedroom by the time I finished the dinner dishes. I would slip out the front door and have a few minutes to join in the baseball game going on out in the street. There were always adults gathered around to watch the children's games. I loved to play softball, except I never learned to keep my mouth shut. I got so excited when I hit the ball; I usually swung the bat and cheered all the way to first base. What I should have learned after a few times was that this gave my mother an excuse to take me into the house as a punishment. She would come to the front door and shout, "Ivy, you make enough noise to disturb the whole neighborhood. Get in this house now."

I cried all the way to her bedroom. I hated walking into the dim, smelly room. I could see Daddy's large frame under the sheet on the iron bed. My mother had begun a new pattern of stepping out of her housedress before standing guard by the door in her torn old slip. When Daddy turned over on the mattress, the metal springs would clank, and I could see the belt lying by him. He began sometimes by just getting out of bed in his boxer shorts and giving me a few lashes around my cotton housedress. Afterward, I began screaming, and Mother made me sit in an oak chair by the Singer sewing machine. She then got under the covers with Daddy, and I waited for my opportunity to crawl out of the room to the cot in the living room.

Then there were the times Dad cross-examined me on subjects I did not understand until in my twenties. Every time I said "I do not know," he wrapped his belt around my cotton housedress until after my siblings had finished their homework, listened to radio programs, and gone to bed. Those nights, I would end up passing out; and the next morning, I could not remember how I got on the cot with Susie.

Some evenings, Dad had me sit in the oak chair by the old Singer pedal sewing machine. If I put my head down on the machine, Mother would scream, "Sit up and look at us!" I would begin crying. "Stop that crying! That gets on my nerves." I would wait until the old metal spring began clanking, slip out of the room, and get on the cot with Susie.

Outside of school and church, my social life consisted of going from neighbor to neighbor, gathering scraps for John's piglet. John fenced it in the lower right-hand corner of the backyard. Because John had the reputation in the family of being bashful and very proud, Mother told me I would collect the scraps two nights a week, which pleased me because I got to get out of the house. After a while of transferring scraps from neighbors' containers into my bucket, I began feeling ashamed carrying a bucket of slop up and down the street as if I were that elderly man who collected scraps in the apartment. However, instead of someone sticking me with a needle, I got kissed!

Mr. and Mrs. Ball and their sons lived a couple of blocks up the street from our house. One evening as I was standing in the kitchen doorway talking to Mrs. Ball as she washed dishes, the front door opened. Her middle son, Glen, came in and, as naturally as if an everyday occurrence, kissed me on the lips, turned, and walked back out the front door. I stood embarrassed, not to mention shocked, and I knew these brothers would tell my brothers.

The next afternoon, I arrived home from school to see Mother and Mrs. Ball sitting in the living room talking. Instead of my usual lingering around, I changed clothes and began dust mopping the floors in the back part of the house. I thought, *If I stay out of sight, Mrs. Ball will not remember to tell Mother about the kiss.* In a flash, I became paralyzed when I heard a group of neighborhood kids, led by my brothers, on the front porch singing, "Glen wants to marry Ivy."

I began crying and ran to the living room, shouting, "Mother, make John and Steve leave me alone." I really did need and like these signs of recognition, but at the same time, I had to prove to Mother that I did not like boys by protesting.

Even though Mother smiled and acted as if it was cute that Glen had kissed her daughter, she used it as an opportunity to have Daddy cross-examine me. The sessions had become intense, my nose bleeding became a common occurrence, and Mother made sure I had a washcloth to hold during the beatings, fading in and out.

During the first and only time I remembered my parents quarreling over something having to do with me, Mother left for a few hours in protest. While cleaning up the kitchen from dinner, I found a two-page letter on the table that Dad had written Mother. After I finished the dinner dishes, I heard those horrible words flowing from Dad's bedroom. "Ivy, come in here now."

When I entered the room, he instructed me to sit in my usual hard oak chair. I sat in the old chair until my body became numb and my siblings had turned the radio off and gone to bed. Dozing, I heard those beautiful words: "Ivy, you can go on to bed."

I heard Mother open the front door. Daddy met her in the living room and accused her, "You smell like beer," and I knew he would call me back into the bedroom. However, they did not call me until the next evening.

When I walked into the room crying, Dad said, "You lucked out last night, but you will not be so lucky tonight."

That night, at nine years of age, I thought, *They both know they are hurting me, and they do not care.*

Being conscious of that fact, I learned to sing in my mind, "Jesus loves me. This I know, for the Bible tells me so." I also tried to pray, but I did not understand why adults bowed their heads and shut their eyes to talk to Jesus. Somehow, just knowing the words to the songs "Jesus Loves Me," "What a Friend We Have in Jesus," and "Bringing in the Sheaves" kept me from getting too angry.

I loved to rock in John's little green rocking chair, holding Granddaddy Ooking's large old family Bible on my lap and singing at the top of my lungs, "Jesus loves me. This I know, for the Bible tells me so."

On one such night, Mother took away that joy when she demanded, "This is the last time I'm going to tell you. Stay out of John's chair, put that Bible back where it belongs, and stop that singing."

However, when I took the clothes off the line in the backyard, I continued my loud singing. I knew our dog, Brownie, loved to hear me sing. He would rub against my legs; and I would lean over, hug him, and sing at the top of my lungs, "And I will come rejoicing, bringing in the *sheets.*" I did not understand the real words: "We shall come rejoicing to heaven, bringing in the sheaves."

Church life became even more exciting when I realized the teenage group had parties with food. I gave up adult choir practice to crash their activities whenever I heard it announced from the pulpit. When I crashed my first Christmas party, I learned that the best time of the year was exchanging gifts. Jeannie, a teenager six years older than I was, drew my name. I ripped the paper, discovered a box that said "one pound of chocolate-covered cherries," and sat staring at the box, wondering, *How will I ever get this into the house without my brothers taking it from me?*

Slowly, I took the lid off to get the aroma of the great chocolate smell. To my surprise, there in green tissue paper I saw a flowerpot with some dirt left in it. Once I got over the disappointment of having no chocolate cherries, the colonial woman with dirt in her apron pocket became a special treasure in my secret hope chest.

I hated the week before Christmas at home. Mother saved that week so I would be there to hand her utensils and wash the pots and pans as she baked. I hated the chore of stirring the homemade chocolate pie filling because, invariably, I let it stick to the bottom of the pan. Then she would fold her index finger under her thumb and flip my head as she screamed, "Dumb Ivy, you let the filling stick. Now let me see you clean this pan!"

I especially enjoyed the Sunday nights at church before Christmas when Santa stood in the foyer giving out candy and fruit. Every year, he allowed me to take to my brothers and sister a treat so they would not eat mine.

Another wonderful, exciting thing about Christmas was that it was the only time of the year I got to go to Granddad Ooking's house. Every Christmas Eve, Susie and I usually received a gold locket or ring with our initials on it. In my third-grade year (it would be four more years before television would be in most homes), our grandparents gave the two brothers one expensive Christmas gift between them: an 8 mm movie projector with Bud Abbott and Lou Costello movies, which brought many laughs into our subdued home when we were allowed to watch.

Every year, Grandmother had the four of us children sit at her feet as she talked of the death of her two-year-old daughter, who had died of pneumonia even before Dad was born. On the return trip home from our grandparents' celebration, my family made remarks about Grandmother having too much to drink, and they did not know if they could take another year of listening to that story! I thought that her little girl dying was the saddest story I had ever heard.

After Christmas, the next great event I looked forward to was in the spring when the teacher took all of us girls to the big brick school building to practice the maypole dance around the flagpole. The night of the performance, I felt beautiful being part of the movements in our pastel dresses and watching the weaving of the colorful streamers over and under. Most of the other girls had parents there to "ooh" and "aah" over them. No one was there for me, and I felt ugly and sad.

Regardless of how I felt about myself, though, I looked for ways to have fun; and toward the end of school, I suggested to the third-grade girls. "Let's have a pet show on Saturday."

The next day, Sally told me, "My mother said we could have the pet show on our large front porch." When I learned that I had to watch Susie that Saturday afternoon, I told her she had to help me get Brownie to the pet show. However, Brownie, with his sleek body and short reddish brown hair, led us to the pet show.

When we arrived on the concrete porch with its four-foot wall, we lined the dogs, cats, spiders, and other insects where they could not get away from us. I could not remember which animals won first place—awarded with homemade construction paper ribbons—but we just had fun sharing our animals and being able to talk without the teacher getting mad at us. Unexpectedly, the pet show had a surprise ending when my friend's mother served delicious refreshments.

Monday at school, we were still excited about the success of our pet show. (On my final report card, Ms. White credited me with much of the confusion that took place in the classroom.)

One of the best memories of my life with this family had to be when Mother invited her mother, Mama, to our house for visits of a couple of weeks. Since her divorce, Mama traveled between her six married children's houses; and when she felt unwanted at one house, she moved on to another.

Mama's visits not only curtailed long sessions in my parents' bedroom, but my grandmother would say the most beautiful words to me: "Run along to school with your friends. I have all afternoon to do the dishes." As I ran for the door, Mother would give me one of those chilling looks, but I knew she would not hurt me in front of her mother.

Mrs. Gray, the widow who lived next door, and Mama taught me that morning glories opened in the daytime and shut at night. I stood on our side of the short wire fence with Mama to watch the multicolored flowers come alive and then close in the evening.

Mama loved to be outside with us children. I would not go in the cold, damp concrete basement because a boy had trapped me a few times and tried to pull my dress up. Nevertheless, some of my favorite memories of Mama were playing church in that basement. We sat on orange crates, our former living furniture, and sang. Mama's favorite hymns were "Precious Memories," "When the Roll Is Called up Yonder," and "Amazing Grace." Afterward, it would be time for Steve to thrill his grandmother with his talent with words.

Once, I volunteered to preach. After all the years I had sat in church, I had memorized all the songs but could not remember one thing the preacher had said in his sermons except the word *sunglasses*. The only reason I remembered that was Mother had purchased Susie a pair of toy sunglasses. Therefore, I stood up on the orange crate and began preaching, "It is a sin to wear sunglasses." My sermon was short-lived when Mama laughed, the rest of the audience hissed, and that ended my career.

I never saw Mother show any respect to her mother as I had to show my parents. In fact, sometimes Mother would be so spiteful, causing Mama to send word for someone in the family to come and drive her to the next one of her children's homes on the list before her time was up with us. When she went out the door carrying her shopping bag of earthly belongings, the four of us would stand on the front porch and cry, "Please do not leave us."

Toward the end of the school year, Patsy, from whom I had stolen the quarter in first grade, gave me her friendship ring to wear overnight. Some of the girls even traded clothes, but even if I had nice things, I knew Mother would not let me trade back and forth. However, when I got home from school and began my chores, Mother spotted the ring on my finger. She promised, as usual, in front of the boys, "When Daddy sees that ring, you are going to be sorry that you brought it home." The fact that Mother called me into the bedroom before I could finish the dishes made me know that meant deep trouble, and I never dreamed how badly.

My parents took their places, and Daddy began, "Why did you bring a ring home that does not belong to you?"

I defended myself through sobs. "Patsy told me I was her friend, and she wanted me to wear her ring overnight."

Daddy replied, "You are never to bring anyone's belongings into this house."

Just as I answered, "Yes, sir," he knocked me back on the bed with the hardest hit I had ever had.

With belt in hand, he asked, "Are you ever going to bring anything in this house that belongs to someone else?"

I cried, "No!" He hit me with the buckle. I screamed. Blood began gushing from my nose, and the last thing I remembered, Mother got into bed with Daddy.

My greed caused my next big nosebleed. Because my friends had balloons, jacks, rings, and candy, I had the nerve to steal a dollar bill from John's treasure chest! I could not remember what I had purchased with the dollar, but I had so much change left over that I became scared. Finally, I decided to dig a hole in the front yard and bury the change.

One Saturday morning, the four of us children were standing on the front porch, watching the spring rain. I ran out into the yard pretending to be digging, and suddenly, I screamed, "Hey, look at the coins I found." Within seconds, we were running in the rain to the little candy store up the road.

Sometime later, John missed his dollar and threw a gigantic fit. I panicked when he began accusing me of stealing his money, and Dad began questioning me about the coins I found in the yard. I confessed a lie, "Mama gave me the money the last time she stayed with us."

The next day, the four of us were home from school eating our lunch when Dad walked into the house. He lied, "Ivy, I drove to see Mama, and she told me she had not given you a dollar."

I fell for his trick, began screaming, and confessed that I had taken the dollar. This time, my parents proved beyond a shadow of doubt that I was a liar and thief in front of the others. In one swift movement, Daddy had his belt in hand and began swishing it around my little cotton-dressed body in front of his children. I never realized anyone could tell that I had been crying until I arrived back at school after lunch and the teacher asked, "Why are your eyes so swollen?"

I lied again, "I burst a balloon, and it hit me in the eyes."

Another afternoon, after arriving home from school, I embarrassed myself by getting caught stealing money. Mother and our neighbor Mrs. Ball were sitting in the living room, and Mother told me, "Go get my pocketbook. I want you to go to the store."

While I was in her room, I took a dime and put it in my shoe for candy and ice cream. Just as I got to the living room door, the coin flew out of the side of my shoe and rolled for what seemed like hours across the hardwood floor toward, of all people, my mother. The humiliation of getting caught in front of the neighbor who liked me made me sacrifice my desires for sweets over stealing again.

During the final week of school, an event happened that placed me in the middle of something a child should never have to deal with. Our dog, Brownie, had been going up the hill behind our house, chasing the neighbor's chickens. One day a man knocked on the door and asked, "Is your daddy home?" Daddy got out of bed, and I could hear the buckle of his belt as he pulled on his trousers. He walked to the door, smiling, and was very cooperative. As soon as he stepped onto the porch, the man introduced himself. "I am the constable, and your dog has been reported several times for killing the neighbor's chickens."

Dad's face turned red, and he told the constable, "I had not been aware of that."

The official replied, "Your neighbors suggest that I shoot him."

The four of us began screaming, running out of the living room to the porch, and begging for a chance to keep Brownie in the yard. The constable replied, "Once a dog begins to kill chickens, it is nearly impossible to break them."

Daddy looked at the boys and told them, "Get Brownie by the collar and bring him here." They refused and ran back to the living room. The dog ran out the street behind Mary's house.

The constable told Daddy, "The dog senses something is going to happen."

Daddy said, "Ivy, go get Brownie."

I began screaming, "No, sir, please do not make me!" Taking only one look at his eyes burning holes into my soul, I knew I had no other choice.

I hated him when he shouted to the boys through the screen door, "Bring a piece of corn bread."

Carrying the bread, I walked down the street, barefoot in a torn old dress, and went behind pretty Mary's house. The dog immediately bounced toward me. I bent over to hug him as I had done hundreds of times while taking laundry off the line and betrayed him with a kiss. Brownie made sad, whimpering sounds and licked my face, and I wiped my tears on his fur as he ate the bread. Then he followed me home. I ran into the house. As soon as the four of us heard the shot that killed Brownie, my siblings began screaming, "Dumb Ivy killed Brownie like she did Blackie."

I sought sanctuary at church by attending the teenagers' events and joining my own age group. I went on their annual hike to Tank Hill. When I was in third grade, I thought my Sunday school teachers, Jean and Dean, were old. I did not realize at the time that they were of high school age. The twins were different in size and personalities, and I loved them equally.

Midmorning, we began our hike toward the west end of town, and I proudly carried my brown lunch bag. I walked between Jean and Dean out the familiar street past Granddad Ooking's store and to the wooden overhead bridge. If a trailer truck crossed, rattling the boards, we would scream at the top of our lungs and laugh as the truck's noise drowned out our voices.

We then continued on a few blocks to an avenue. The group again stopped to view a two-story brick house under construction, which looked out of place on the street of one-story white-framed houses. I became bored and puzzled by the amount of time spent looking at the unfinished house. Finally, I got the nerve to ask, "Why are we walking around this house?"

The teachers turned, stared at me, and replied, "You do not know where we are?"

I answered, "Why, no!"

"Ivy, do you not know that your granddad is building this house for your family!"

Years later, I would learn that this deal was struck in Baltimore when my grandparents came after I had been raped and my parents falsely accused an innocent man. For the last three years, Granddad Ooking had kept us in rented houses until he could build the family home. I also learned that he gave me lifetime rights to the house.

I would have another hurdle to get over before we arrived at the large water tank: I would have to walk a log across a creek. I had not had many opportunities to play, and I was not as flexible as the others were. I watched everyone scale the beam before I told the leaders, "I will have to sit here and wait for you to return."

My leaders pleaded, "Ivy, please at least try sitting on the log and scoot across." Until that moment, I had not realized I was the only girl in a dress. For years, I had wanted a pair of jeans like those that Susie wore to play. I will never forget the first pair of jeans I ever wore.

One Saturday afternoon, I was left home to care for Susie. I put a pair of John's jeans on and went outside to jump rope with my friends. In my delight, it never dawned on me to watch the time for John's return; and when he caught me, I spent the evening with Mother and Dad in their bedroom.

Anyway, to please my teachers, I straddled the log in a dress, and it took me at least ten minutes. By the time we arrived at Tank Hill, the other children had signed their names on the tank with lipstick and were ready to eat.

When I got back to church, I ran all the way home to surprise my mother with the news about the big brick house. However, when I walked in the door, she surprised me by saying, "We had strawberry shortcake today, and I saved you a serving."

I sat at the table smiling, lapping up the dessert, and felt safe to say, "Granddaddy Ooking is building us a big house."

Mother gave me one of her spine-chilling looks and snapped as she went out the door, "I know that!"

After the screen door slammed, I heard her say to the boys on the front porch, "Poor Dumb Ivy."

Most Saturday afternoons after lunch, since Daddy and Uncle Bob only worked half days at Granddaddy's building supply shop, they disappeared for the weekend. Usually, I sat and watched Mother and her children playing games, or the children would grieve with her that Dad had not come home.

I celebrated my tenth birthday with Mother staying in bed and crying because Daddy had not come home the night before. Naturally, I had many chores to do; and when I took the trash to the barrel, I heard Mother talking to my brothers. "Take the money Granddaddy Ooking left for her birthday gift and get a little girl's pocketbook."

When my brothers passed me on the back steps, they teased, "Goody, goody, you do not know where we are going!"

I bit my tongue to keep from shouting. "You think you are so smart. I know you are going to buy me a pocketbook." I knew Mother would cancel the gift if I lost my temper with her sons.

To my surprise, my brothers bought a beautiful little girl's brown leather pocketbook. I opened it to find a card that read, "To my daughter." Tears filled my eyes when I saw the card had not been signed.

Suddenly, I thought of Mrs. Gray and ran next door to show her my beautiful birthday gift. She complimented the gift and invited me to carry it to her church for a revival that evening. I ran back into the house where Mother was still crying over Daddy and softly asked permission. To my shock, she stopped crying, got out of bed, and stated, "We all will go." As Mother, Susie, and I walked down the avenue toward the Church of God with Mrs. Gray, I watched how the two women carried their purses and positioned mine the same way.

In contrast to my life of abuse at home, I learned to relax in the safety of the people at church. Therefore, at ten years of age, when some people in the congregation of the Church of God began standing up, clapping their hands, and singing, I did not react because, in my little world, the only place no one had ever hurt me was in church, my sanctuary of relaxation.

The next week, I could not wait to get the breakfast dishes done to show off my new purse as an upperclassman in Mrs. Hare's fourth-grade class. The two fourth-grade classes were still in the annex building, where I had been in the third grade the year before. In contrast to the unsettling year before, I was thrilled to discover that my new teacher's schoolroom had an atmosphere as if soundproofed with a peacefulness, which enabled me to leave all my troubles outside the door. I took the first seat in the second row to be near Mrs. Hare as she taught interesting subjects.

Especially during the first week of October, I felt myself floating in the ocean blue with Christopher Columbus as his fleet—the *Santa Maria*, the *Niña*, and the *Pinta*—left Spain on August 3, 1492, for a test run. Right in the middle of learning that Columbus accidentally discovered America, my teacher threw me into a tailspin when she announced, "Monday, we will learn about Columbus's return trip home with the *Santa Maria* out of commission. Also, this is Ivy's last day with us and let her know she will be missed."

Unknown to me, on Monday morning, Mother planned for Susie and me to walk to a new school with John and Steve. She instructed me, "At lunchtime, find Susie's room and bring her to the new house for lunch."

I enjoyed the march along the street with my elder brothers even though we felt as if it were a funeral march, leaving friends and familiar places on the east side of town. We crossed over the bridge to the west end of town. John led us straight up Main Street and past the old apartment over the Farm Bureau. In a couple of blocks, he turned left, and—surprise—we headed to the school with the big bell on top.

When the four of us arrived in front of Nob School, the students were already in their proper lines. The four of us stood alone when I heard someone say, "Ivy, what are you doing here?" Joanne, my long-lost first-grade tap dancer friend, put her arm around me. "I remember how scared I was the first day when I arrived here. I will introduce you to Mrs. Ward, our teacher."

When I got settled into my new schoolroom, the classroom rumbled with the noise of oak chairs hitting against the oak floors as students moved about. Another distraction was that the long wall was lined with large windows, and the bright light caused my eyes to burn and water. Oh, how I missed the cozy classroom I just left behind.

When I got through the first morning of the new school, at lunchtime, I found Susie in her third-grade classroom. Confusion multiplied. Mother had instructed me to bring Susie home at lunchtime, except she did not give me directions to the new house Granddaddy Ooking built.

Susie and I agreed to follow the majority of the students down the two flights of steps and out the front door. Of course, we should have gone out the back door. We turned left, and of course, we should have turned right.

We walked up and down streets as fast as we could for forty minutes of our lunch hour. Finally, I approached a woman cleaning out her flowerbed, and she told me of the only new house she knew, four more blocks out her street. We arrived for the first time at our new home with only ten minutes left of our lunch hour. Mother screamed, "Where have you been, Dumb Ivy? Are you so dumb that you cannot find your way home?"

She instructed Steve, "Teach Susie how to find her way to and from school." I followed close behind as he walked to school in five minutes. At the end of the day, I felt secure knowing that I only had to go out the back door and walk two blocks home.

I lived in a world of abuse and did not adjust well to changing homes, churches, and school locations. Moving from east end to the west end of town, I went from a leader of the pack to the low man on the totem pole. I did not know how to fit in with the different style of dressing, whispering, passing notes, and being in a clique.

Additionally, when it came to math, I remembered how my teachers at the other school would not allow anyone to disturb the class. Now I understood why. I could not understand what my new teacher explained during math class because of the distractions around and about me. The prospect began looking brighter when the teacher chose me to help grade the class math quiz. Since coming to Nob School, my obsession of being chosen by the teacher to grade papers outweighed learning the subjects.

Once, when I graded the math paper of the smartest boy in class, I put a red *X* mark by a wrong answer. I looked over at Clyde with the red hair and thick magnifying lenses in his glasses, and I felt sadness for him. Therefore, to keep from hurting his feelings, I changed the red *X* to a check mark. When the other helper saw what I did, she rechecked my change and shouted to the teacher, "Ivy changed a wrong answer for Clyde and made it correct."

My face flushed when the students began chanting, "Ivy loves Clyde," and that ended my grading papers for the teacher.

At the same time, things at home began deteriorating for the whole family, and I did not care how I fit in at school any longer. Since first grade, I had wanted to know what it would be like to take my lunch to school. It was not long after we moved into the new house that I finally got my wish, and it was not pleasant, to say the least.

I came home from church one rainy Sunday afternoon and opened the front door, and I could smell the tension in the house. I walked to the kitchen door, and there stood Mother crying while frying a skillet of potatoes. I went upstairs to find Dad searching through closets. By the time I changed clothes and went back downstairs, Dad had the buffet drawers open in the dining room.

Just as I asked Mother, "What do you want me to do?" she bellowed out a scream, picked up the cast-iron skillet of potatoes, and threw the skillet upside down on the floor. As she ran up the steps, she shouted threats at Dad. "I've had enough of you tearing through this house looking for money, and I am leaving."

Especially during the weekends that Uncle Bob spent away from home, Mother and Daddy would wake us children in the night with terrifying loud quarreling over money. I could remember one horrendous argument when I heard Daddy say, "I will go and ask Ivy."

When I heard his steps, my heart skipped a beat; and for once, Mother came to my rescue when she cried, "If you will go out to the car, I will tell you about Granddad Ooking's money for Ivy."

Unbelievably, this rainy Sunday afternoon, Mother came down the steps and went straight out the front door with suitcase in hand. While leaning over, picking up potatoes from the kitchen floor, I heard the front door slam. I went to the kitchen window and watched Mother until she turned the corner and walked out of sight. Immediately, Susie began screaming, "I want my mother!"

I mopped the kitchen floor, John and Steve went to their rooms, and Daddy got in his car and left. Later that night, I heard Uncle Bob come in the house from his weekend off and John telling him, "Mother has left us."

The next morning before Daddy and Uncle Bob left for work, Daddy instructed me, "If your mother does not come home by the time school is out today, I will take her picture to the police so they can find her."

The word *police* brought back the fear of going to the police station in Baltimore. In my panic-stricken state, I cried, "Do you have to talk to the police?"

He never answered. He just continued. "Here is money for you to buy Susie's and your lunch."

At lunchtime, Susie and I followed other children to the local restaurant, climbed up on spin-around stools at the counter, and ordered hot dogs for each. While the other children ate, we sat there with tears dropping on the uneaten food and fretting over what would happen at home.

Two evenings later, Daddy informed us, "I have given the police Mother's picture, and they have not found her yet." Then he made the strangest suggestion to us. "If you would rather not have Mother come back, I will hire a nice redheaded woman to do all the chores and take care of the family."

When Susie would not stop screaming for her mother, Daddy promised, "I will go to the house of Mother's sister and bring her home."

I lived to regret the decision that I had not voted to bring the redheaded woman to do the chores of a nine-room house because, upon Mother's return, she added housecleaning to the chore of doing the breakfast dishes before I could leave for school.

At the top of the stairs was a bathroom; and to the left were the two bedrooms where Steve, Bob, and John slept. To the right was Susie's and my room, right across from our parents. Mother coordinated my schedule so cleverly that Daddy and Uncle Bob never suspected I was the cleaning lady.

Every morning, Mother motioned for me to follow her downstairs to start breakfast while Daddy and Uncle Bob dressed for work. When they came down for breakfast, I went back up to make their beds while my siblings dressed. I made seven beds and dust mopped four bedrooms, the hallway, and the steps. Then I ate my breakfast and washed the dishes, which left me fifteen minutes to dress and get to school.

At lunchtime, after Daddy and Uncle Bob ate and left for work, I washed the dishes, which gave me five minutes to be in homeroom before the tardy bell rang.

After school, I finished dust mopping through the living room, dining room, and front and back bedrooms and cleaning the downstairs bath. Afterward, I had to iron or dust until it was time to begin dinner. Then Mother let me sit down when it was time for the men to come home so they would see me doing nothing until it was time to wash dishes.

Mother was successful in isolating me from the family so that I was not even aware that anyone could hear me when I began talking to the dishes. The unfairness that my siblings could walk to school with their friends in a relaxed mode made me angry. So when I washed dishes, I even made sure the utensils felt important by washing them in the order I put them in the dishwater. If I washed one out of its turn, I apologized, "Oh, I'm sorry you lost your turn."

One evening while washing the dinner dishes, unknown to me, our grandparents had come into the living room. After finishing the dishes, I walked into the living room, and my grandmother asked, "Where is your little friend?"

I said, "Excuse me, Grandmother?"

She replied, "I heard you talking to someone in the kitchen."

Mother skillfully chimed in, "That's nothing new. She is always talking to herself."

While Grandmother and Granddaddy Ooking questioned her indifference to my abnormal behavior, Mother gave me one of those looks that made my stomach hurt, and I took the opportunity to fly out the back door to join the baseball game already in progress in the field.

I had on an old red two-piece dress someone had given to Mother and a pair of wedge-heel shoes. I still smacked the softball, boys and girls had to dodge the bat as it flew into the air, and I slid into first base like a lady. However, as soon as my grandparents' car backed out of the driveway, Mother called from the back door, "Ivy, get in this house. I'm tired of hearing your mouth."

Since moving to the new house, my parents never demanded that I come in their bedroom as they had years before. However, just about as cruel, they made me come upstairs and sit in my room across the hall from them. I climbed the steps crying and shouting, "It isn't fair the other children get to stay outside!"

My parents would demand, "Go in your room and stay there." It was futile to plead my case by comparing myself with their children.

The first time they called me to my room, I came up the steps crying, walked into my hot bedroom, and slammed the door. I braced myself when I heard Daddy's feet hit the bare oak floor. Fortunately, he just pushed my door back and, with great restraint, reprimanded, "You are never to shut this door ever again."

I hated sitting in my room listening to the sounds coming from my parents' bedroom while the squeaky bed sounded as if it would fall. I sat on the footrail of my bed and continued to watch the ball game out the window. After a period of silence, Daddy walked down the hall in his boxer shorts and went to the bathroom. After all the years of being in their room, I did not know where I got the idea that Daddy went to the bathroom because of urinating on his wife.

At other times, when I would be too upset to watch the game out the window, the only comfort I could find was to lie at the foot of the bed, talking to the picture of Jesus hanging on the cross. I had torn the picture from my Sunday school book, stuck it in an old frame, and hung it over top of my bed. I could not look at the picture without crying because the mean men had rejected, beaten, and hung Jesus on a cross.

Periodically, Susie would lie at the foot of her twin bed, and together we would cry because Jesus had nails driven into his flesh. Anytime Susie and I would begin to get close, Mother destroyed any chance we had of improving our relationship by commenting, "Susie, don't listen to Dumb Ivy."

On long hot summer days when I was supposed to be cleaning the upstairs, I would talk to myself in the mirror of the bathroom medicine cabinet. While my friends dreamed of becoming movie stars, I had secret talks with God in the mirror. Repeatedly, I would say, "I wish that I could have been the mother of your Son, Jesus." Other times, I acted as if I were a schoolteacher by imagining rows of children and watched the expression on my face as I talked and laughed with my class, not realizing anyone in the house could hear me.

Now as I looked back, if I cleaned the upstairs before leaving for school, why did Mother let me take all morning upstairs after school was out for the summer? I begged to go outside to play with my siblings and the neighborhood children, and she totally denied my request. The beginning of absolute loneliness in the upstairs under Mother's total control had some of the same effect as when I used to be in her bedroom; my nose would bleed from aggravation and stress.

That same fall of 1948, when we moved to the new school and house, I had to give up relationships that I had depended on for emotional support for the last three years at the Kee Street Methodist Church. The crushing blow came—as usual, very unexpectedly—when Mother demanded, "Go tell the twin sisters that you will not be walking to church with them any longer."

I did not care what happened to me; I went into screaming fits. "But why?"

For once, Mother explained something to me: "Beginning this Sunday, you children will ride the First Baptist Church bus where Granddad Ooking attends."

I walked two blocks to my twin Sunday schoolteachers' house. They opened the door and invited me to come into the living room.

Before I could sit down, I began crying and stuttering. "I cannot walk to church with you any longer." The two sisters sat on each side of me on the couch. One wiped my tears while the other one pulled my hair back out of my face before asking me why I could no longer walk to church with them.

That next Sunday morning, the four of us climbed aboard the big yellow church bus. As fate would have it, just as the driver pulled into the intersection, the twin sisters came around the corner and began the half-hour walk across the wooden bridge to Kee Street. I could feel the hot tears running down my cheeks as the driver continued driving uptown. I never told Pastor or Ms. Johnson good-bye or saw them again.

When the bus stopped in front of the First Baptist Church, I walked into my new Sunday school class, and there sat my tap-dancing friend, Joanne, and three other best friends from my new fourth-grade class at Nob School. For the first time, I began associating and identifying with my own age group.

After being at the new church for only a few weeks, the bus stopped running, and I began walking to church alone again. Fortunately, as at the Methodist church, I found acceptance by many loving women.

I immediately loved the gentle Mrs. Byrd, who had been the leader of the Junior Girls' Auxiliary (GA) for many years. I joined the girls who assembled every Wednesday afternoon after school. I met girls from three different grade schools at the GA meetings at the church, listened to missionaries' stories, and worked on requirements in the Forward Step program. However, it was not too many weeks until I paid more attention to Terri, who went to another grade school and was one year ahead of me in school.

The first memorable event was when Terri went from princess to queen in the Forward Step. At her candlelight coronation service, I fantasized about being a queen as I watched her walk down the aisle in a long white dress. After the placing of a crown upon her head, she recited 1 Corinthians 13, the love chapter from the Bible. I made a vow to myself, while listening to her, that I would become queen someday and recite that same chapter at my coronation service.

When school let out for the summer, Mrs. Byrd invited the GA girls to meet in her elegant home. During these summers, I observed every little detail of Terri's actions. One afternoon, she stood with perfect posture and shared a mission story. I watched her lips form every word she pronounced precisely, and I wanted to stand and sound just like that.

After the meetings, Mrs. Byrd invited us grade-school girls to sit at her large formal dining room table for juice and cookies. Instead of joining in conversations with the schoolgirls, I took every chance to snitch another cookie off the china platter. Even with my bad manners, I never once saw Mrs. Byrd show signs of disapproval toward me. In fact, if I missed a meeting, there would be a card in the mail saying, "We missed you at the meeting and hope to see you next week." In addition, if she heard that I was ill, she would knock on my front door to visit me, even bringing a gift!

These types of visits were hard on Mother. When anyone from the church knocked on the door, if possible, she would have one of the children answer and say, "Mother is not in."

The few times Mrs. Byrd visited, I wished that we could have served her refreshments in return for what she gave me. However, very rarely did we have anything besides soul food.

When we first moved into the new house, Mother made sure that the four children experienced the weekly grocery shopping and had her list memorized. Upon entering the A&P, the first item was a twenty-pound bag of potatoes to be placed at the bottom of the grocery cart. Then on to the buttermilk, butter, eggs, fatback for seasoning pinto beans, three two-pound bags of pinto beans, five pounds of sugar, a box of loose tea, Eight O'Clock coffee, seven cans of Carnation milk, ten pounds of flour, five pounds of cornmeal, maybe kale or hominy, and miscellaneous other items of soap or Duz for washing clothes as specified. Every week, Mother checked the items against the register reading to make sure that we had not sneaked any goodies to eat on the way home.

One Saturday, Susie and I spied the one-pound aluminum pan of chocolate and vanilla fudge, which had its own plastic knife. There was no way we could resist that much candy for 19¢. Knowing there was no way we could eat all of it before getting home, we decided to begin eating while gathering the items on the list and pay for it at the end.

Shopping for the heavy items seemed easier as we walked through the aisles laughing and eating chunks of fudge. One thing was for sure: the manager knew where we were at all times in his store, and once we entered the checkout line, he would call a taxi for us. However, it was common knowledge that I had a problem around dark uniforms, such as taxi drivers and elevator operators, and it was a given that Dumb Ivy would not ride a taxicab, so I walked home while Susie rode.

Anyway, this particular Saturday, by the time I arrived, my sister looked relieved that Mother had not come down from her bedroom, and Susie had put away the groceries to keep Mother from checking the items against the receipt. Susie and I ran next door to join the ball game in progress, and that brought Mother out of bed as she called me upstairs to my bedroom.

Oh, how I hated it when school ended, and I was confined to the hot upstairs. My best friend in the neighborhood lived across the street with her mother, daddy, and dog. Sally's parents worked and gave my pretty brunette friend pretty dresses and *two* bicycles and left her home alone to come and go as she pleased. Whenever I heard the dog bark or the metal gate shut, I would run to a window to see if Sally was coming or going, who her new boyfriend for the day was, and what short outfit she wore. From the open bedroom window, I could listen to the neighborhood children cheer on their team as they played softball in the vacant lot next door.

Through the years, many children had run from base to base, which left a permanent diamond pattern deeply imprinted in the ground. The sunken lot helped to make the sidewalk a nice long bench for spectators to sit and watch the games. If there were too many players, the extras usually shouted to borrow someone's bike.

On Saturday afternoons, I gladly did the lunch dishes since that began my free afternoon. I spent many hours holding on to Sally's fence while trying to balance myself on the older of her two bicycles. The afternoon I finally had the nerve to let go of the fence, I asked Susie, "Would you like for me to double you?"

She had enough confidence to climb on the seat behind me and stand as I began pumping, and the bike began wobbling with the extra weight. By the time we turned left at the corner grocery, I lost control and dumped us both head-on into the storm drain ditch. Once we landed, we began laughing so hard that the teenagers from the ball field had trouble pulling us out of the ditch.

However, an exception to our Saturday afternoon freedom came close to my eleventh birthday in 1949, when our parents put us children in the car and drove to a nearby town. Daddy parked on the steep side street beside the sanitarium and took John and Steve into the laboratory. While they were gone, Mother turned and explained to Susie and me, "If you promise never to tell anyone about this trip, Daddy is going to add an additional quarter to your weekly allowance."

Upon hearing this, immediately, my sister and I became excited and planned to go to a movie when we returned to town, and Mother did not object. In a short time, Daddy and the boys returned to the car, and Mother ordered Susie and me to follow her. We walked into the building right off street level. I saw people in white and became hysterical. Mother grabbed me with the assistance of a nurse, and I got my shot. To this day, I did not know why we had the shots.

At the beginning of the next week, for the first and only time ever, Mother let me choose my school clothes from the Sears, Roebuck & Co. catalog. Every school year, Mother traced each right foot of each one of us on large brown grocery bags and mailed them with the shoe orders. During the fifties, a majority of people wore their clothes until they were threadbare or outgrown, to be handed down to another member of the family. I loved the first day of school when just about every student showed off their new outfit that had to last for the rest of the year.

However, when I entered Mrs. Ball's fifth-grade class wearing my new dress, there were butterflies fluttering in my stomach. I had heard of stories of how strictly my new teacher conducted her classes. I needed Mrs. Ball the year before when I arrived at this new school because I had become stone-deaf to anything a teacher taught in class. After welcoming us to her class, Mrs. Ball gave out the list of books and dismissed the class to have time to collect used or new books we would need for the next day.

This was my family's first year in the neighborhood, and on the way home, sixth-grader Sally shared the neighborhood tradition: "The gang meets at the ball field, and we all go door-to-door and help each other find secondhand books to purchase."

I ran into the house, shouting, "Sally asked me to go with her to search for my secondhand schoolbooks."

Mother demanded, "Give your list to your brothers, change clothes, and get to your chores."

For the rest of the day, I slipped by the windows to see who had gathered back at the field. Even when there was not a ball game in progress, usually, a dating couple would be sitting on the sidewalk. Finally, my brothers, Susie, and friends gathered back to brag of their book find and have an ice cream from the corner grocery. The frustration of being excluded brought forth blood from my nose as I watched the festivities in the neighborhood without being able to participate.

In reality, I would have been just as well off staying home as going to fifth grade. By the time I arrived at school, not only did I smell sweaty from the housework but I also had to run fast to get to school before the tardy bell rang. I had no idea what the teacher talked about on any subject. Nevertheless, it gave me time to relax and daydream. I let my mind wander as I dreamed of what it would be like to have pigtails, pretty dresses, and boyfriends like Ashley, the most popular girl in our class. She had chosen me as her best friend. I could not understand why because I was not one of the top students.

No doubt, Uncle Bob had become disappointed in me since changing schools. Thankfully, he decided to nip in the bud my frustration with fractions and bought an orange and apple. I had trouble comprehending that 1/5 (which had the number 5) was smaller than 1/3 (which had the number 3) until my uncle cut the orange in five pieces and an apple in three chunks. It did not take long before I knew that I would rather have a chunk of the apple rather than the smaller piece of orange.

As I progressed through school, not only did the math become harder but also the spelling words. I usually ended the evening in tears because Uncle Bob insisted that I write the ones that I could not spell ten times each. By test time on Fridays, I made good grades on my tests, which gave me self-respect with my good friend Ashley. The only thing I had in common with my new school and the one that I had left was that I became alive at recess.

My favorite game, red rover, proved to be the catalyst that totally shattered my self-confidence for the fifth-grade year. Two lines would stretch across the road about fifteen feet apart, facing each other. One team would sing, "Red rover, red rover, let Scott come over." Scott would back up to get a good run, and the line that sang the challenge grasped hands to keep him from breaking through. Scott would decide which two people he thought would be the weakest link in the line before running toward them. If he broke through, he came back to his team. If he failed to break the hands, he had to stay with the opponent's team.

The day I heard my name, I backed way up and ran as hard as I could. Two girl friends thought it would be funny to let go of hands just as I got there. I ran way past them before landing on all fours on the pavement. The scrapes and bruises didn't hurt nearly as much as revealing the hole in the heel of my sock. I was wearing my mother's gray suede wedge-heel sandals, and when the buckle broke, the strap around the ankle revealed a hole in my sock.

I sat in the middle of the street, bleeding and trying to keep my hand over the hole. The teacher asked my good friend Ashley to walk me home. As a result of the fall, my teacher sent a note to my mother, "Please do not send Ivy to school wearing heels again."

As usual in my short few years on this earth, another situation was waiting to take me by surprise. The afternoon the teacher took the fifth-grade class across the hall to the library to watch a documentary on West Virginia's conservation, I sat on beside of Ashley with her boyfriend. During the movie, I felt my underclothes becoming damp, and I asked permission to go to the bathroom. When I sat on the toilet, I became horrified at the sight of blood on my panties. Of course, I had never heard of the monthly menstrual cycle, and the beginning was a mystery to me. My mind raced back to the time my parents accused a boy of putting a hole in my snowsuit, and at all cost, I would have to keep this a deep, dark secret.

I outlined my stained underwear with little squares of rough school toilet paper and went back to my chair in the library. I looked over at the beautiful fresh, clean Ashley holding hands with her handsome, well-dressed boyfriend. I was very much confused when the menstrual cycle arrived repeatedly.

However, spring arrived, and Mrs. Ball had a wonderful reputation for her springtime activities. Every year, she let her class choose a spot among her former classes' trees and plant a tree before she gave us ice cream. In addition, at the end of the school year, Mrs. Ball took our class to the movie theater on Main Street, along with the two other grade schools in town.

The three schools packed the movie house with nonappreciative students of literature to see, of all movies, *Julius Caesar*. During the classic movie, popcorn flew through the air like snowflakes, students mocked the acting, and I laughed until my sides hurt. Those were good spring memories to make me laugh as I began spending long hot days in the upstairs of the house when school let out.

There were men at Granddaddy's building supply shop who could have painted the walls in the house, but Mother insisted that she and I could do it when school let out for the summer. I became very angry when she would not use the drop cloths, which Daddy brought home with the paint and brushes. I had to sit on the floor with a gallon of turpentine and rags to wipe up every spot of paint that she dropped on the oak hardwood floors.

Finally, the project was over, and I hoped for some freedom, but she assigned me the job of cleaning the hardwood floors downstairs with Varsol and thick Johnson paste wax. Since we did not have a buffer, I got to skate in old socks to shine the floor.

During these projects, Uncle Bob approached his sister on my behalf. "Ivy will be in sixth grade, and she doesn't know the multiplication tables. Will you let her take a couple hours a day to write them?" Mother agreed with her brother, and he continued. "I want Ivy to write each line of the multiplication table one hundred times."

When I heard that, I popped up off the floor and chimed in, "Do I have to write the 1s?"

Losing patience with me, my uncle shouted, "Yes, write the 1s one hundred times."

That evening, Uncle Bob came home from work with notebook paper and pencils for my long journey through the multiplication table. Every day, I counted down to Wednesday afternoon when I got a break to go to the GA meeting. Mother might not allow me to play in the neighborhood with her children, but she had to let me go to church to keep in good standing with Granddad Ooking.

To my knowledge, no one at school, in the neighborhood, or at church knew of my abuse unless there were signs observed unknown to me. The fact that I had never been taught about personal hygiene like the other children would have caused suspicions.

God used those Sunday mornings, Sunday evenings, Wednesday GA meetings, and Thursday evenings' choir practices to shield my lonely journey on earth. Now in my seventies, I could honestly say, "Thank god!" If Mother had allowed me to be part of the gang in the neighborhood, it would have been my nature as a preteen to choose playing ball over attending church. The adults there helped me cultivate strength through the teachings of Jesus, forgive others, go the extra mile, and do unto others as I would have them do unto me.

I still had to depend on the song "Jesus Loves Me" for daily strength when away from church. Unbelievably, in all those years, I never heard that Jesus suffered, died, and resurrected for my sin nature, that he died for me personally.

When we sang the GA hymn, "We've a Story to Tell to the Nations," I sang at the top of my lungs while wondering, *What is the story we are to tell?* One afternoon, I decided that, whatever it was, I wanted to go to Africa and tell the story. I knew the older girls let the pastor know when they were ready to give their lives to full-time Christian service. That gave me the idea to go tell the pastor that I wanted to be a missionary. The next Sunday, I asked Pastor Cox, "May I come and talk to you?"

Immediately, he answered, "How about tomorrow at noon?" He made me feel so important by his quick response.

Monday, washday, Mother and I took clothes from the soapy water and put them through the wringer of the washing machine. I made sure they fell in the tub of clean rinse water, which sat under the wringer on a stool. Then Mother ran the clothes back through the wringer from the rinse water. I caught them, placed the clothes in a basket, took them to the backyard, and hung them on the line. By then, it was time to empty the tub of soapy rinse water, fill it with clean water, and begin again with the next load.

Nervously I kept watching the clock. I did not want to miss my appointment with my pastor. Nor did I want my mother to make fun of my decision to be a missionary because every time I mentioned the name God in the house, she acted as if I had used a dirty word.

At eleven thirty, with one more load of laundry rinsed and lunch ready for Daddy and Uncle Bob, I blurted out, "Mother, I have an appointment with Pastor Cox at noon. May I go?"

It took her by surprise; she nodded yes as she continued taking clothes out of the soapy water and never asked why. I ran like blazes up the steps, put on a skirt and blouse, and ran all the way to church.

I felt too small for the secretary to announce to the pastor that I had arrived. Nevertheless, he came out, took me in his office, and motioned for me to sit in a large leather chair in front of his desk. I scooted up in the chair, where my feet did not touch the floor, and I felt important when he questioned, "Ivy, what do you want to talk about?"

I smiled and informed him, "I want to go to Africa and be a missionary." He gave me a big smile of approval and words of encouragement to follow God's leading in my life. For the first time in my life, I listened as someone prayed to God for me, even using my name.

I felt special for a few Sundays until a tall, dark, and handsome man in a dark business suit stood in the pulpit as a guest speaker. After church, I heard my pastor calling me. I turned, and he pointed to the professional-looking man standing in the foyer, greeting people, and insisted, "I want you to talk to him. He is a missionary."

Up to this point, I had only seen smiling women as missionaries in our GA manuals. I thought, *If that distinguished man is a missionary, then this little girl could never be.* As soon as the pastor turned to walk back toward the man, I ran out the side door of the church and didn't stop running until I got home. After that, I cooled the idea of going to Africa and began concentrating on my social life as time neared for me to enter sixth grade.

Another event I had to endure every Saturday morning was watching out the upstairs window as my brothers, sister, and the neighborhood kids met at the ball field and walked together uptown to the 5¢ western movie at the local theater. I stood holding the dust mop watching the girls in their blue jeans and pretty blouses chase boys until they turned the corner out of my sight.

However, I would forget about the movies when, on Sunday mornings, Eliz welcomed me to sit in church among her four children. Many Sundays, she invited me to take a Sunday afternoon ride with the family. After church, I would run home, wash the dishes as fast as lightning, and run to my friend's home. After a pleasant afternoon, I would run home to wash the dinner dishes and afterward run back to church for evening training union and Sunday night church service.

Life in our small town had settled into a routine since the end of World War II until the summer when family life was interrupted abruptly with President Truman giving permission to use ground forces in Korea. General MacArthur began an increase in the fighting forces against the trained North Korean People's Army.

Our hometown veterans had worked hard to get their careers and families reestablished after returning from World War II, and suddenly, some of them vanished from their homes to the hot, muddy war zones of Korea. The Korean War became a reality for me one Wednesday afternoon when I was walking down on Main Street after a GA meeting. Bill, one of the ballplayers, walked toward me, carrying a duffel bag. I knew he had gotten his call because he reminded me of Uncle Bob leaving for World War II.

In 1950, at the ripe old age of twelve years, I began sixth grade. My new teacher this year, Ms. Tabor, insisted that we give reports on the Korean conflict. My report was that, during the summer, the North Koreans' army had burned Seoul, and the Communist flag flew over that capital city.

The war news infiltrated the group of my intellectual sixth-grade friends. At recess, instead of playing our favorite games, Ashley and I debated the pros and cons of the Korean War, mostly with the boys. In the evenings, families began sitting around their radios again, waiting for any news of the *war*.

I decided that we needed friendship not only in the world but also in the group of girls at Nob School. The grade schools did not have social clubs as in high school, and I had a plan to form a friendship club. Two girls volunteered to help me write invitations on three-by-five index cards, inviting all sixth-, seventh-, and eighth-grade girls to become members. A seventh-grade friend suggested, "How about using my basement as a clubhouse?" She lived a couple of blocks from me, I had free time on Saturday afternoon, and that settled the meeting place and time.

After a few meetings, I became discouraged when the girls agreed that there would be no more open invitations and that no one could become a member unless voted in by the majority. They also voted to change the club's name from Fellowship to the Yellow Jackets and decided to purchase jackets.

Surprisingly, Mother agreed that I could purchase a $12 club jacket with the money Granddad Ooking had given her for my birthday. Proudly, I joined my friends at the sports shop for the purchase of fifteen yellow windbreakers with "Yellow Jackets" embroidered in black thread across the back. The popularity of the jackets brought many requests for membership, and many were denied. This accomplished the exact opposite of what I had set out to do and caused a larger division in school.

Being in sixth grade, I had to learn to listen to more than one teacher. Besides my homeroom teacher, I would have Mrs. Swain's music class, Coach Walter's physical education, and Mr. Bolton as our bandleader. I desperately wanted to be part of the band outings. In contrast to my friends who played small lighter reed instruments and could read music, I had to use the abandoned trombone of my father and brother.

I found out not only that I could not read music but also that only boys sat in that section of the band. Just as lost in band as in school, I did learn the seven slide positions of the trombone, and the teacher marked the numbers on my music sheet 1 through 7.

Since Jim sat on the first chair, I found it easier not to look at the music sheet and move my trombone slide when he moved his. I watched Ashley and other friends marching out in front as majorettes and flag girls, and I felt "manly" being the only girl in the big horn section.

My one big and only trip with the band was when we marched at a bridge dedication in a nearby town. I dressed in Steve's white slacks, white shirt, and gold tie. He had to teach me how to tie the knot in my tie. I was unprepared for the uproar when I walked out of the house. The ballplayers began a round of wolf whistles until I walked out of sight. Now I understood why John carried his uniform to school and dressed there rather than walk through the neighborhood.

That Saturday, I had my first experience of marching and trying to keep my eyes on where Jim moved his slide. Now that was a one-woman slapstick comedy in color.

After the parade, all bands were given free time, and the small town swarmed with little band people. I felt awkward with most of the band people except for Ashley. She and I went to the five-and-dime, where we met some of the girls who excitedly displayed their new rings, tangy lipsticks, candies, chewing gum, and Blue Waltz perfumes.

They challenged us to see if we could steal a ring without getting caught. Well, for me, it seemed everything I did had a way of finding its way back to my dad and his belt. I had never forgotten the whippings he gave me when I stole or brought someone else's belongings home. The fact that I was with the most popular girl in school made me feel confident in saying, "No, thank you," to our school friends.

However, Ashley did not react out of fear of her parents as I had. She just clearly stated, "My parents do not allow me to steal." Our fellow band members rolled their eyes at one another as if they had just met up with two girls from outer space.

In other ways, unknown to her, Ashley introduced me to another side of life. Once, when teachers sent us to town to run errands, my friend saw a three-quarter-length gray tweed coat with a faux fur collar in the window of the exclusive Mademoiselle shop. For the first time, I entered the beautiful store and watched Ashley try on the pretty coat. Oh, the next day, we girls went crazy when my friend wore the tweed coat to school.

On another errand we ran, I stood with her in front of an exclusive shoe store, drooling over a pair of sling-back flats displayed in the window. The next day, Ashley wore a pair of black ones with heel taps to school. I loved the way she sounded walking down the hall, and she told me that for 50¢ the shoe shop would put a pair on my shoes.

Ashley had taught me that the monthly period was normal to all females and something to be proud of, as we had become women. I had kept my secret for well over a year and still could not share it with anyone. Oh, how I longed for Ashley's security when she shared with me, "Mother called Daddy at the office to bring home a box of sanitary napkins."

It so happened that, right after that, Mother cornered me in the kitchen and began, "You are old enough to have begun menstruating. If you do not begin soon, I will have to take you to the sanitarium for a checkup. Once you begin, you will need sanitary napkins."

Anytime she cornered me, whispering, I felt dirty. To add to the confusion, the terms *sanitary* and a *sanitarium* frightened me. I heard that sick people went to the sanitarium—or was it *sanitary*?—and I did not want to visit a doctor. Somehow, something triggered my mind as to what she must be talking about, and I couldn't wait until the next time so I could share my secret and not have to go to the doctor.

Thursday evening, getting ready for choir practice, it happened, and it took every nerve in my body to call out from the bathroom, "Mother, will you come here?"

When she opened the door, I was sitting on the commode, and I pointed to the blood on my panties. She smiled and said, "Oh, just a minute."

I heard ripping sounds, and then she returned with a pad made from a torn sheet and instructed, "When you begin, you have to stay in bed for a few days."

I begged, "But I don't want to miss choir practice tonight!" She let me go on to church, and the next day, I had to stay in bed while she went to town to purchase my first and only box of napkins. From that day forward, it was up to me to handle the problem the best way I could, like I had been doing for a year.

At the same time, she threw her old pink bra at me, which I had played with for years when shut up in the upstairs. I had come close to getting caught wearing that pink bra outside the house.

Mother and Steve had taken the train to Cleveland to see the Indians play in the World Series, and Mama stayed with the family. What a vacation that was for me because Mama would say, "Now, Ivy, run along and play with pretty Sally, and I will do the dishes."

The morning Mother and Steve were to return, Mama asked me to walk to A&P for groceries. I ran upstairs and put the pink bra under a sheer white blouse, and since it had no hooks, I used a gigantic safety pin as the bra's clasp. I walked up the street leaning forward so that the blouse would press against my back and everyone could see that I wore a bra. After getting a large brown bag of groceries in my arms, I leaned forward and began walking down the street when I heard my name. I turned and saw Mother and Steve a couple of blocks behind me. I ran home in record time and changed clothes. When Mother arrived, she asked, "Why did you take off running?"

I lied, "I had to get the groceries to Mama before you got home."

Now that I felt older and more mature, I wanted to be a lady. I dropped out of band and joined the school choir. However, I still could not read music; and unknown to me, I could not carry a tune. Anyway, I felt at ease with the beautiful, dark-eyed, black-haired, and soft-spoken music teacher, Mrs. Swain. It seemed obvious to me that she liked us students. I also loved the crazy songs she taught us: "I went to the animal fair. The birds and bees were there. The big baboon by the light of the moon was combing his auburn hair. The elephant sneezed and fell on his knees, and that was the end of the monk, the monk."

I remembered well the one song that she sang every class that I actually hated, "Oh My Darling Clementine." Whenever we sang, "Were number 9 . . . boxes without topses, sandals were for Clementine," I stuck my feet under the chair because I did not want my friends to tease me as my family loved to sing, "Dumb Ivy, if your feet get any larger than these size 9s, you will be wearing the boxes."

In the midst of playing at being a lady, the physical education coach treated me as if I did not exist and showed partiality to the petite girls who were not afraid of gymnastics. I rolled forward into a crooked somersault to pass his class until it came time to form my homeroom basketball team. He coaxed me into joining Joanne and Ashley as team guards, and we had the best three forwards any grade school could have. We were just unbeatable, and some upperclassmen who had successfully achieved the state basketball championship would pass me in the halls and say, "Hey there, Mark Workman." He was a player for West Virginia University.

At the time, the comment crushed my spirit because I thought they were telling me, "You are a big, fat girl who looks and plays ball like a boy."

As I looked back to those early years, the boys could have possibly been complimenting my abilities and wanted to befriend me. The words "There goes Mark Workman" rang negatively because I had spent my childhood with family members continually making cruel remarks. Therefore, I imagined compliments from outsiders as making fun of me. I did not know which hurt worse, the words from the basketball stars at school or the songs Mother taught my brothers to sing: "We don't want her. You can have her. She's too fat for me. She's too fat. She's too fat for me." To be honest, I must have needed to lose weight, but I did not get as much to eat as the other family members.

By the time I was in fourth grade, Granddaddy Ooking had Mother put me on a diet of wheat toast and boiled eggs. Since Daddy had been the only person eating sliced bread in our family, I thought it must be serious since I had to eat store-bought bread instead of Mother's homemade biscuits and corn bread. I did not understand what a diet would do since I was not conscious of a physical body until an uncle met me on the street and commented, "Ivy, you look great since losing weight."

The colorful new life of spring became the brightest spot of life after a winter of blizzards and the Korean conflict until the worst humiliation of my school years occurred. It happened when our music teacher, Mrs. Swain, substituted while our teacher, Ms. Tabor, took a few days off. The fact that our class did not fear our music teacher made us misbehave badly, to say the least. Some of us girls tried to help Mrs. Swain by asking everyone to settle down. Just before the end of the day, the teacher, at her wits' end, declared war on the class by making the comment, "The very next person who makes one sound will get paddled."

This harsh statement from my favorite teacher shocked me because I had never so much as heard her raise her voice. I thought, *Surely she would not paddle any students. I will just try and see.*

I hid behind Louise, who sat in front of me. In the silence of the room, I made a short low grunt, and students turned, pointing at me. They chanted, "Mrs. Swain, you promised to paddle the person who made the next noise."

Her face turned red without her sweet smile, and she said, "Ivy, come up front."

Five minutes later, the dismissal bell rang, and students ran out in the hall where the eighth graders were coming out of their class, shouting to my brother, "Your sister just got a paddling."

I ran home feeling stupid and began my chores. When Steve came running into the house, he shouted, "Mother, Ivy got a paddling in school today for making a noise."

My stomach churned as I waited to hear "Just wait until Dad gets home." Instead, with relief, I heard her just say, "Poor Dumb Ivy."

Later, Mother called me to set the table for dinner, and Steve blocked the doorway, talking to Mother, and I said, "Please let me by." Steve raised his hand and slapped me right across the face. I began screaming until I looked at his mother, who gave him a smile while continuing to mash the potatoes.

When Ms. Tabor returned to class, she made a mysterious announcement. "This afternoon, the principal wants all the sixth- and seventh-grade girls in the gym." This created an air of excitement until it was time for us to line up single file into the gym and select our places in folding chairs positioned in a circle. The suspicion grew until the woman from the 4-H organization introduced herself as one on a mission to choose the best-groomed girl in the school to enter a county competition on Saturday. Naturally, all eyes turned to the popular Ashley, who would not only win the county title but also go all the way to state against any other girl from anywhere. To me, I thought the happy Ashley who had two blond pigtails and blue eyes, was of average height and slim, wore the latest fashion, and was a cheerleader was the perfect specimen. The only thing anyone could have against her would be jealousy.

I saw antennas going up as girls began competing against my friend for the honor as the 4-H representative called each name off a chart. She rated each one of us on nails, hair, posture, and so on. Afterward, the representative and teachers spoke in confidence to add our scores. I sat and watched the popular girls eyeing one another as time came to announce the winner. However, instead of hearing the name Ashley, I heard her say, "Ivy is the winner of the best grooming contest."

I knew this had to be a bad joke. But once the reality of the honor sank in, it was not the girls' approval I needed but Mother's. *Finally, she will see that I am not so bad after all.* I ran all the way home and shouted before I got the front door open, "Mother, Mother, I won the best grooming contest at school today!"

She gave me that horrible look that made my stomach hurt and shouted, "Do not ever come in this house screaming like that again! Go change your clothes and begin your chores."

When I had changed, I slowly walked back down the steps and said, "Mother, I am to go to the park on Saturday to compete in the county for best grooming. I want to wear my maroon taffeta Easter dress and my navy blue wedge shoes."

She glared at me and replied, "Absolutely not! You know that park is too dirty to wear good clothes."

Saturday morning, I finished the breakfast dishes and my mother instructed, "If you have to go to that park, wear your white nylon blouse and black taffeta skirt."

I begged, "Mother, please don't make me wear that sheer blouse because my pink slip will cause me to lose the contest. I only have a pink slip."

I had the choice to stay home or wear what she demanded. When I told Mother I had to walk to the post office to ride to the park with the representative, she burst my bubble by saying, "You didn't win because you are the best but because the leader is good friends with Granddad Ooking and Martha," who was my real mom.

This time, as I walked up the street, I did not lean forward as I had the time with the pink bra. I hoped that by standing straight as a board, no one would see my pink slip shining from under the sheer blouse. And the confidence I'd had by winning over all the girls at school disappeared with Mother's news that I didn't win on my own, and the old Dumb Ivy complex returned to go with me.

When my age group paraded around the stage, my heart felt like it broke when the winner wore the exact same dress that I wanted to wear, only in navy blue, and she wore the same style of shoes. I ran to the parking lot and hid behind a car to cry, and the winner walked by, surrounded by family and friends congratulating her. To add insult to injury, as I walked back into the building, the woman who had selected me said, "It will be late this afternoon before I will drive back into town. Did you bring money for lunch?"

I answered, "No." She handed me a quarter, and I drowned my sorrow in a hot dog and drink.

We arrived back at the 4-H office after five. I walked home feeling defeated and hopeless. I entered the house, and Steve asked, "How did you do in the contest?"

Angrily, I looked at my mother and felt the hate as I shouted, "The girl who won had on an outfit just like I wanted to wear. I could have won the county title."

When I saw the mocking look on my adoptive mother's face, it reminded me of the disgusting looks she had when anyone spoke of my real mother being homecoming queen in high school and at college. "Goody, goody you didn't win." She went back to listening to the update on the Korean War and left me to deal with the silent, helpless war raging within me.

Dealing with Mother was not nearly as difficult as facing my friends back at school on Monday morning. The hardest part of not winning was when the girls gathered around, asking, "Did you win the county title?" That had been my one and only big break to become a leader since coming to this new school. At least I didn't have to worry about anyone being jealous of me.

On the last day of school, another announcement had me gasping when Ms. Tabor explained, "If you do not get your report card, please stay. Everyone else is dismissed to have a great summer."

I sat in my seat feeling every bit the old Dumb Ivy as our classmates filed out the door. Of course, they turned to see two people who had goofed off all year and me sitting and listening to the students snickering, "You've failed! You've failed!"

After the students left, I sat at my desk staring out the window and trying to imagine the horror of facing the world now that I had failed sixth grade. The mystery ended when Ms. Tabor said, "You three students please come up front to my desk." She handed each one of us a large envelope. She whispered as if we held the top secret of the government. "I did not want the other students to know that the office secretary missed sending your school pictures back to the company and that you can have them for free."

The three of us could care less about the pictures. Our eyes were fixed on the three report cards on her desk. Finally, she handed them to us, and we ripped into our report cards and immediately looked on the back at the wonderful words, "Promoted to seventh grade."

However, I hid my report card from the two boys standing nearby, even though their report cards were even worse. I felt stupid when I saw that I had made Cs in every subject because I could remember the wonderful feeling when I made As and Bs the first three years at the previous school. Worst of all, I did not know how to ask for help.

Steve graduated from eighth grade that year and would join John in high school the next school year. During their years at Nob School, I had been popular with the upper-class girls because they wanted to meet my handsome brothers.

However, one Sunday evening, one of John's old girlfriends came close to giving me a nervous breakdown because I had never been able to say no. I was walking on Main Street toward the church for the evening Baptist Training Union (BTU) when this beautiful high school majorette approached me. "There is plenty of time before BTU, and I want to treat you to a Coke."

At first, I felt honored that this high school girl wanted to buy a grade-school kid a Coke. Therefore, for the first time, I entered the forbidden high school hangout, the Honey Bee, and felt important sitting in a booth sipping a Coke with this popular girl, that is, until her boyfriend slipped in the booth beside her and his friend sat beside me. When the friend tried to begin a conversation with me, I spoke up, "It is time for me to leave for church."

As I fled, the high school guy shouted, "I will give you a call." At times like these, I was thankful that my family had never had a telephone installed in our home.

The next Sunday evening, to my surprise, Alice waited to tell me, "That guy really did like you. My boyfriend and I want you two to double-date with us."

For the first time, I did not care if I hurt someone popular or not; my fear shouted out directly, "Never! Do not ever ask me again." She did not! She never spoke to me again!

Periodically, close friends did call me on Mrs. Mann's telephone, and I loved an excuse to go to her house to play with her baby boy. Some Saturday nights, she styled my hair, and I paid the 50¢ fee by babysitting while she did chores. Every time I returned home from the neighbor's house, Mother and my brothers sang, "Knock her down again, Pa. Knock her down again. She's been telling the neighbors all about our kin."

I would cry, "Mrs. Mann is too nice to talk about anyone."

However, I did notice a big difference in her good life after a spring revival with the evangelist Eddie Martin. A large tent was erected in the vacant lot in town, and all three grade schools and the high school bands took turns playing for services. The night our band played, we missed the preaching because we had to take our instruments back to school after playing for the hymn singing.

The next day, I tried to figure out what had happened to family and neighbors the night before at the tent meeting. I knew only what Susie told me. "Many people went to the altar. I stood holding on to the folding chair in front of me until my knuckles turned white to keep from walking forward. I told myself that being in the fifth grade is too young to go forward."

I found out that five neighborhood families, my two elder brothers, and many school friends had gone to the altar on the night that I missed. I could not understand why going to the altar caused these people to begin going to church. I had never been to the altar, and I loved being at church. It further surprised me when the Mann family began driving to my former beloved Kee Street Methodist Church.

Another thing that puzzled me was that my eldest brother, John, began reading a little black Bible. This was the first time I had ever seen anyone mark in the precious book, and I would sneak into his room to read the words that he had underlined in red! I had been going to church since I was eight years old and had not learned of a transformation to a new life through the shed blood of Jesus. In my ignorance, I figured these people were different because of baptism.

I walked the church aisle quite by accident one Sunday morning when a high school girl could not find anyone else to go forward with her. The next Sunday, the pastor baptized us, and I felt special when I came out of the church; and for the first time, Granddad Ooking waited to drive me home. I wished that I had listened to what he had to say to Mother when he went in the house to talk with her.

What surprised me was my mother would not let me play with my friends in the ball field. However, anytime I had chores finished,

I could dress up and attend tent revivals by myself. I spent many a spring and summer evening sitting in tent meetings during grade school and high school years.

One hot evening, dressed in a blue and white polka-dot dress, I walked out the street and entered the tent where the Karl family from Ohio held a two-week revival. The highlight of the evening came when their good-looking grown son used cowbells to play beautiful old hymns. Every night, Pastor Karl preached on the Antichrist, who would come and deceive the world. At thirteen years of age, I had no fear of the devil or hell. In my thinking, I had never hurt anyone as my parents had made me suffer. Therefore, I felt my parents were bad, and I had confidence that I would be in heaven with Jesus when I died.

Many nights, I prayed, "Now I lay me down to sleep. I pray the Lord my soul to keep. If I should die before I wake, I pray the Lord my soul to take."

After praying it twice, I would say to Jesus, "I am sending one for tonight, and the other one is to be applied when I die." It would be a long journey before I would come to know that Jesus died on the cross for my sinful nature, which knew how to steal ice cream and candy.

Another reason I did not fear death was that anytime a neighbor died, my mother would send me in her stead with a large Hershey's chocolate cake. She instructed me to serve coffee and cake to the mourners who sat up all night and to keep the dishes washed. I loved being in the kitchen with some of the neighborhood women as we sampled foods the neighbors brought to the house.

It was customary for the coffin to be set by a window in the living room of the family home with a semicircle of folding chairs in front of the casket where family and friends volunteered to sit all night. Periodically, I would walk around the circle and whisper to each person, "Would you like coffee or something to eat?"

By daylight, I would go home to rest. Later in the morning, Mother would send me back to clean the house when the family left for the funeral and help the women have a meal on the table by the time the family returned from the cemetery. I was confident that standing in for Mother developed compassion for ones who suffered as I had.

Once, when Mother stood guard at the bedroom door and Daddy was whipping me with his belt, I found myself sitting on a green hillside in peace. I looked to my right, and there stood a shepherd nearby holding a staff, and I relaxed completely in his presence.

In another instance, which I had taken for granted until fourth grade, we were reading a story of beavers building dams. I raised my hand and told the teacher, "One day I sat in a bright green forest at the edge of a river and watched the beavers carry wood to build a dam."

One of the intelligent students shouted, "That is impossible because beavers are not common to this area." Not only did I relax in the vivid, colorful forest where the beavers were not afraid of me but a bright light shining to my right also shielded me to feel safe and peaceful.

As I waited to become a teenager that August, Mother ordered school clothes from Sears, Roebuck & Co. To pay for my clothes, Mother demanded that I wax all the furniture and the floors, clean the windows, and scrub all appliances in the kitchen and bathroom. In the hot, sweltering house, I cried and pleaded, "Please make Susie help me. She is always outside playing."

Thankfully, I finished the projects before Sunday because, when I came home from church, John and his girlfriend, Betty, invited me for a ride in his 1947 Chevy for ice cream and to celebrate my becoming a teenager.

Since Betty always looked cool and neat in the hot summer, I ran to the back porch to polish my white shoes before getting in the car. John drove around town for a while before stating, "Let's go back by the house and see if anyone else wants ice cream."

Once home, he instructed, "Ivy, go in and ask if anyone wants cake and ice cream."

I stepped inside the door; and Ashley, Jill, Sally, Joanne, and ten other school friends shouted, "Surprise! Happy thirteenth birthday!"

Mother gave me one of those looks that made butterflies flutter around in my stomach and scolded me in front of my friends, "When you cried because Susie did not help you clean house, she was running around town giving out invitations for your surprise birthday party Granddad Ooking planned for you."

During the opening of the wonderful gifts, my grandparents arrived to meet my friends. The short happiness ended when Steve brought me to tears by an open assault in front of my friends: "You acted so surprised, but you knew about the party because I saw you polishing your shoes."

As we began preparing for school, an open assault by the First Marine Division in Punchbowl filled the radio waves. By the time I began seventh grade, the Korean War was in full-fledged fighting, and the marines had reached Soyang River north of Punchbowl. My seventh-grade teacher did not have as much interest in the war as she did in English and literature.

What a surprise! For the first time since leaving my previous school, I began learning again. I could still see the words *have*, *has*, and *had* written on the blackboard as helpers for *seen*, *been*, and *done*. The teacher took an interest in me and suggested that I read biographies of Helen Keller, George Washington Carver, and Booker T. Washington for extra credit in literature. By the end of the first semester, I had suffered through the lives of someone besides me, enduring tribulations and hardships.

Another good aspect of seventh grade was that Ashley and I were special friends without excluding anyone. She invited me to help her serve refreshments at her mother's garden club. The best part of the fall meeting was that it would take place at Ashley's summer home on the lake. My friend's father, brothers, and their friends had gone the day before us to open the home and do some fishing. Ashley; her younger sister, Sally; and I arrived the next day with my friend's mother.

By Saturday afternoon, everything was ready, and we had time to play before bathing and putting on our best dresses. We ran through the woods with her brothers and their friends, where I learned I could not handle isolation. Not far from their home stood an abandoned house, and Ashley's brothers told spooky stories about the place before inviting us to enter. Everyone ran to enter except me. Just to confirm what a nice person my friend was, as badly as she wanted to run with the rest, she replied, "Ivy is my guest. I will go back with her."

At the time, I did not have the verbal capability to express my fears about going into the spook house. To add to my embarrassment, I could not share my bathroom needs with anyone, and I did not have the nerve to tell Ashley that I had to hurry back to the house because of diarrhea.

After taking a bath, I hid my sordid underpants in a brown bag. Then I slipped on my new red corduroy dress that Granddad Ooking had given me the month before for my birthday. Ashley and I had a great time serving the garden club members.

Unfortunately, Monday, after that special weekend at her summer home, Ashley missed school. Without warning, I experienced firsthand some girls saying malicious things about my special friend. The main thing that seemed to bother the gossipers was that Ashley began the school year wearing not one but five beautiful different-colored pleated plaid skirts with matching crewneck sweaters. These girls cornered me, saying, "You know that Ashley's father did not buy her new clothes while traveling. They came from a rummage sale."

I became frustrated in trying to defend my friend by saying, "It doesn't matter where her outfits come from. She always looks pretty."

Running from these gossipers, I ran head-on into Ashley's younger sister, Sally. After we talked of the fun weekend we had had at their summer home, I blurted out, "I hope your sister is coming back to school tomorrow. There are girls telling me that your dad bought Ashley's new skirts and sweaters from a rummage sale."

The smile on Sally's face changed to horror as she replied, "He did not!" and ran from me.

The next day, my best friend returned to school and embarrassed me when she handed me a brown bag. She let me know that I had left a pair of sordid panties at the summer home and that her mother had washed them for me. Then very clearly, she stated, "I trusted you as a true friend until you talked about me to my sister." That was it! There was no second chance even when I begged for forgiveness.

Ashley and I remained casual friends through the rest of grade school, but it was not the same as when we used to share our dreams and secrets with each other. I loved and respected Ashley so much that I had told her, "If I ever have a little girl, I am going to name her after you."

That winter of 1952, the Korean conflict was not going any better than my social life at school. The months were filled with artillery and air campaigns launched against the Communists. In addition, General Ridgway left for Europe to replace General Eisenhower as NATO commander at Supreme Headquarters Allied Expeditionary

Force (SHAEF) because Eisenhower gave in to the continual pressure to try to win the Republican nomination for president. Ashley ended the seventh grade disappointed in me as her best friend; however, she did allow me to campaign "I Like Ike" with her.

By summer, the Korean conflict made about as much sense as the conflict in our home. I could not understand why Mother did not acknowledge me as a member of the family. During adolescence, I had a keen awareness of my need of a nurturing mother. This desire deepened when I awoke in the middle of the night to see Mother holding Susie in her twin bed. These times usually occurred after I was awakened in the night by our parents arguing.

The one and only way I survived that life of rejection was by singing "Jesus Loves Me" and "What a Friend We Have in Jesus," cheering me and protecting me from depression. However, there were times when I let my guard down and forgot to run away from the chaotic situation with Dad and my siblings.

Dad always began these sessions by saying, "I'll stand for all you children." The others jumped at the opportunity to gang up on him while I stood back in a corner, watching. The laughter, fun, and wrestling match eventually found its way toward where I stood. Dad swooped me up as he walked toward the front door with the other children hanging on to him, opened the door, and pretended to throw me outside. The whole time, his large hands were tickling my body as I screamed hysterically. After the rowdy and boisterous minute, Dad shut the door, put me down with a sad look on his face, and walked up the steps.

This event ended the same way every time with my siblings singing, "Old Dumb Ivy always ruins our fun with Daddy."

One evening after such an episode, Mother got my attention real fast when she shouted, "If you do not stop that crying, I will have to tell Granddad Ooking you cannot go to the GA camp."

While I was getting ready for my first time at the GA camp, the neighbors were having their difficulties. They were concerned about their loved ones patrolling the boarders in Korea during the July and August heavy rains. That July also brought excitement at the Twenty-Fifth Republican National Convention at the International Amphitheater in Chicago, Illinois, by the nomination of Dwight D.

Eisenhower of New York as the presidential candidate on the first ballot. Since I had heard Mother and my brothers speak of him during my early childhood years of World War II, I thought of him as a member of our family.

At the beginning of August, Granddad Ooking gave Mother the money to buy my camp clothes. We sat with the Sears, Roebuck & Co. catalog. I cried when she insisted on ordering a two-piece blue-and-white checkered bathing suit for me to wear at the GA church camp. "Mother, all the other girls will all have one-piece bathing suits. Please do not order the two-piece for me!" She did!

Remembering all the times Mother talked of how cheap girls looked in scanty clothing, I was brought to tears when she hired a neighbor to make me one set of short shorts and halter for my summer outfit. Now she expected me to go to church camp as the only one in a two-piece suit, and I felt cheap.

I forgot about the two-piece bathing suit when I climbed into Mrs. Gray's car to ride to camp. There were two carloads of giggling girls slowly making their way southward on a very narrow, winding road up and down mountains. Once we arrived in the area, we stopped for a picnic.

While the two women put the food on the picnic table, we girls excitedly talked ninety miles an hour. Mrs. Gray interrupted our chitchat with a statement, which I had never heard or known how to handle. "Ivy has a sunny disposition."

Being the first compliment about my identity, I blew it badly when all I could think of was to say, "Hey! You want to use the food I see under the table?"

Mrs. Gray replied, "Now, Ivy, that was not nice."

In my early years in the church, God always had peaceful, loving, and inspiring women leading me—women I looked up to and wanted to grow up to be like, being a leader as they were. That was something I would have never learned in the ball field, looking back at how God used the church to raise me. Now as an adult, I realized Mother did a marvelous thing by keeping me in the upstairs away from the things teenagers loved to experiment in the world.

When we arrived at the Cedars camp, it most certainly lived up to its name! We entered the circular drive around the cabins. Both sides of the road were shaded with good-smelling tall cedars. Right from the beginning, I fell in love with my pretty blond counselor, Nancy Clay, from Waynesboro, Virginia, who told me something that I had never heard: "I am engaged to be engaged!"

Every night after dinner, there were events of competition among the cabins. One afternoon, Nancy asked me, "Will you play an oriental woman in a skit, which I have written for tonight?"

When I replied, "I would love to," she asked, "Do you think your mother would mind if I cut your bangs to play the part?"

Since I cut my own hair, I said, "Of course not!"

Nancy fixed my hair and makeup, wrapped my body in fabric, and coached me in acting. The competitions between the cabins were judged on originality.

My nerves were on edge because, just before school let out for the summer, I had been the only student in my classroom without a part in the school play. The seventh and eighth graders were downstairs practicing the school play, as Louise and I were the only two not chosen. A boy came to the door of our homeroom to announce, "Ivy, the teacher wants you to try out for the part of the cowgirl."

I hated to leave Louise, but I jumped for the chance to be part of the group. Never having been in a play and never having anyone to tell me what to do, I began reading in a high-pitched voice. I could hear my friends snickering in the background when the teacher insisted, "Go back to class and send Louise."

I watched as the teacher worked with Louise, making her the star of the show and popular with the group. Now just two months after being the only person not to participate in the school play, I became a hit at church camp by winning the skit.

During the fun week, one problem was that I had to be the only girl in a two-piece bathing suit. I ran as fast as I could, jumped into the pool, and hoped the water hid the fact that I was different.

Nevertheless, Nancy changed my life that week by cultivating my talents. She also chose me to give the thank-you speech for the camp director at the last night's banquet. She spent our rest periods coaching me on how to write and give a speech.

Sadly, the last morning at camp, standing out front waiting for Mrs. Gray to arrive, we hugged our new friends, cried, and signed one another's autograph books. As we waited for our ride, we did not know Mrs. Gray could not return for us. I would never forget the humiliation and terrible shock when my mother stepped out of Granddad Ooking's car. She gave me one of those looks and, in front of Nancy and my friends, shouted, "You have gotten fat, and you look ridiculous with those bangs!"

The first day home, my brother shouted, "Ivy, clean the bathtub!"

As I cleaned, I heard Mother tell Susie, "Don't cry. We will picnic again when Dumb Ivy goes to the country to visit for a week." While at camp, the family had vacationed at home with picnic-style meals and left the housecleaning for my return.

I turned fourteen years old with my neighbor Sally treating me to an afternoon movie where we saw newsreels of the Korean conflict. By the time school began, the air force and navy had begun bombing with accuracy. In the heavy fighting, the men on the ground were defending the outposts in Korea.

At the same time, my long-awaited dream of becoming an eighth-grade upperclassman and being the one chosen to pull the rope that rang the bell on top of the Nob School building happened. The first day of school, I began asking for a turn. "Now that I am in the eighth grade, when can I ring the bell?" The day that I stood beside the principal in the stairwell, pulling the rope that rang the bell, calling the children to line up to come in for classes, I thought of being five years old and sitting by the kitchen window over the Farm Bureau, hearing the large bell gonging.

Another change was that my homeroom teacher and math class would be with Coach Walter, the tall shouting coach constantly teasing or trying to embarrass one of his pets. I did not have to worry in that area. However, to save face with my friends, I had to get at least a C average from him in math because any freshman worth their salt took algebra instead of freshman math in their first year of high school.

Ashley decided to take the first seat in the second row, her desk butted up against the teacher's desk because she did not want anything to distract her from learning. Ham sat beside her, I sat behind her, and Brut sat behind me. Ashley, a school cheerleader; Ham, a basketball star; and Brut, the team manager felt secure with Mr. Walter.

Again, this year, the four of us continued the political debates, especially on the upcoming election year for president of the United States and the issue of ending the Korean conflict. One morning as Ashley turned around to share a current event, Brut—who loved to tease until he wore your patience thin—kept tapping my shoulder. He kept repeating my name. "Hey, Ivy. Hey, Ivy."

I politely asked him, "Please wait a minute and stop hitting me."

He began pounding harder on my shoulder. I turned, swung, and caught him right in the face; and his glasses went flying. He looked stunned! I looked shocked! Brut lived across the street from the back of the school, and we usually walked out the door together—except that day. He frightened me when he warned, "My mother will come out on you and make you buy me a new pair of glasses."

I was again thankful that my family did not have a telephone when Brut was not in his seat after lunch and students were shouting, "Brut and his mother are in the office, talking with the principal." When Brut returned to class, I sat waiting to hear my name over the loudspeaker to come to the office to see the principal. Nothing!

After a few days had passed, when Brut began thumping on my shoulder again, I realized that I was not going to get in trouble with his parents or the principal. Because the coach looked up and saw Brut pestering me, he stated, "Brut, are you trying to get Ivy to break your new glasses?"

Not long after waiting for the principal to call me to the office over the intercom, his voice came over. "May I have your attention please? The following people please come to the office: Ivy . . ." I began shaking until I heard Ashley among the other six names. We entered the office marching single file, and the principal solved the mystery. "I had a call from the election board requesting to handpick students to work election polls." I immediately volunteered to stand a block from school and hand out "I like Ike" flyers.

Late in the evening, the election polls closed, and I rushed home to hear Mother's approval that I had worked for her man. The family sat around the radio, and I waited for someone to ask me about my politicking. Nothing! I broke the silence. "Has Ike won yet? We sure were busy at the polls."

Without looking up at me, Mother snapped, "Be quiet. We are listening to the news, and get the dinner dishes washed."

After getting the kitchen cleaned up, I walked up the steps, looking back down at the family, which excluded me, and went to bed. It felt great getting in a warm bed after spending the day in the cool weather when, suddenly, I felt as if I were floating on a cloud and began to doze. It reminded me of the nights when Mother gave us children a spoonful of medicine followed by a spoonful of Ann Page Strawberry Preserves. When I got in bed, the medicine always made me sense the room slowly expanding and then everything coming toward me as if to close in until I fell asleep.

The 1952 presidential election revealed the uneasiness of the American people when Eisenhower received 33,778,963 votes. One reason for the restlessness was that, at the end of World War II, an unspoken cold war had developed between the United States and Russia, and the world's superpowers were facing each other in the Korean conflict. This year for Christmas, the gift most Americans wanted was for our men to be back home from Korea. The winter weather had slowed the action, and by the end of the year, the Republic of Korea had taken over half of the front line.

Days before the January inauguration, I came home from school to find one of the top two greatest experiences of my short lifetime—our family's first television set! There sat a ten-inch screen housed in a cabinet so large that it took two men to carry it. Daddy or one of my brothers had to go out in the backyard every ten minutes and turn the antenna until everyone screamed, "Hold it there! The snow is cleared enough to see the picture."

Two days before the January 20, 1953, the inauguration of Dwight D. Eisenhower, I made a deadly announcement to my school class: "My daddy bought us a television." Since there were only three or four students who had televisions in their homes, the teacher told me, "Great, I will assign some students to come to your house to watch the inauguration."

My stomach felt as if hundreds of cocoons were turning to butterflies as I walked toward home after school. *Fear* rallied in my stomach of what would happen when I told my parents that I had told the class about our television set. We were forbidden to have friends in the house. I would never forget what happened the last time I told about something Dad bought.

For the first time ever, on July 4, Dad brought home a watermelon and three flavors of soft drinks. Susie and I were sitting on the side yard, waiting for our parents to give out the goodies. The neighborhood was unusually quiet until one family came out of the house. Just before they got in the car, the woman shouted, "What are you doing for the Fourth?"

At once, Susie and I began shouting about the items in the kitchen, only we added, "We are waiting for Mother and Daddy to get out of bed."

Boy, did we get instant fireworks. Mother came to the bedroom window and shouted down at us, "Why do you insist on letting the neighbors know our business?"

Then Daddy came to the window and demanded, "Go into the kitchen, get a bottle to drink, and come back and sit in the yard where everyone can see you."

For the first time in my life, I cried because someone forced me to drink soda. Susie and I pleaded, "Please, Daddy, do not make us." When threatened with the belt, we sat in the yard holding a bottle of soda, crying.

That memory haunted me as I walked into the house and decided not to tell my mother about classmates coming in until Daddy and Bob came home for dinner. I stretched the truth as if the teacher had asked me where I would be watching television, and I had to tell her we had one at our house. To my surprise, my dad defended me by saying, "That is all right if the teacher wants to send students." Dad really cared about his reputation in the community, especially with our schoolteachers.

As Dad prepared for our nine student-guests, he discovered that the farther back we were from the snowy ten-inch screen, the better the picture looked. Therefore, he placed the television in the downstairs back bedroom. When my friends arrived, Dad placed fifteen people in the doorway of the front bedroom. We were bumping heads, trying to get a view across the small hallway, as General Dwight D. Eisenhower became the thirty-fourth president of the United States.

Also during this time, our school choir had prepared for the annual county spring festival in a nearby town. Before the concert in the evening, the grade-schoolers from around the county had packed a large school stage for a morning practice. Lunchtime came, and I hurried off with three of my friends to find a place to eat since the restaurants, drugstores, and sidewalks were crawling with students. My friends and I were lucky to find a table where we enjoyed a hot dog when I thought I heard my dad's voice saying, "Ivy."

My heart missed a beat when I saw him standing by the table. The shock of seeing him confused me because we had traveled by school bus, and I could not understand how he knew how to find us. He gave us that sickening smile, which made me wish I could scream, *Leave us alone!*

Then he offered me a dollar to treat my friends to dessert. I mumbled, "No, we've had enough." He slipped away in the crowd as fast as he had arrived.

That same spring, there were other events that took me by surprise. The Yellow Jacket Club sponsored their first boy-and-girl party, and the popular game "pleased or displeased" was the first on the agenda. A person went around the circle and asked each individual, "Are you pleased or displeased?"

One student said, "I am displeased! I want Ivy to kiss Greg." Now Greg—a tall, dark, and handsome upperclassman and obviously an experienced kisser—took me into his arms and gave me my first real kiss in the mouth. The group screamed and shouted when I stumbled back to my seat in a daze.

Just two Saturday nights later, our youth group at the church sponsored a scavenger hunt. I became excited when I saw that Jill's boyfriend had brought his cousin Seth. Even though the cousin was a high school sophomore, Seth and I teamed up with Jill and Doug to run around town going in and out of businesses and friends' homes looking for items on our list. The first team to bring back all the items on their list was the winner.

Afterward, when Seth asked if he could walk me home, I panicked and quickly lied, "I'm going to Jill's house."

When we arrived at my friend's house, her mother greeted us, "Would you children like something to eat?"

Oh, how that impressed me! If only my mother would let me bring friends home. However, instead, I sat watching the clock and wishing the boys would leave so I could go home. I knew Mother would be angry because I was already two hours late.

My mind thought of the times my mother accused me of being with boys instead of being in church. Now if I showed up with a boy, she would convince my siblings that I had been out with a boy instead of being at church. The later it got, the more panicked I became and did the unthinkable—I asked my friend to go home and spend the night with me. Her mother just smiled and said, "Sure, and I will see you children in the morning at church."

The four of us walked in the middle of the street one block away from my house, and I saw one of Granddad Ooking's lumber trucks turn the corner. It stopped. John opened the door and shouted, "Get in!"

The truck was too high for Jill and me to get in, and as the boys pushed us, I heard Seth say, "I will need a ladder to elope with Ivy." The fact that I brought Jill home with me made Mother so angry that she never mentioned the subject of the boys.

After church the next day, while sitting on the front doorstep, I heard a loud motorcycle. It turned the corner, and I froze in place as I watched it come to a stop right in front of me. The person took off his helmet, and there sat Seth in broad daylight. I was alone with a boy, and before Mother and Daddy found out, I tried to be polite by asking him to leave. Susie came around the corner of the house, blowing Steve's baritone as the cycle fired up and went back around the corner.

Added to the spring craziness, two weeks before graduation from eighth grade, the principal announced, "Anyone who would like to go to the circus tomorrow will be dismissed for the afternoon."

My new friend Maggie, who had moved to town that school year, agreed to go to the circus with me. I rushed the dishwashing, hurried out the street, and turned the corner. I heard someone say, "Hey, are you on your way to the circus?"

On the corner of the avenue was a two-story country home, which had a porch that circled three-fourths of the house. Recently, an elderly couple had moved in, and I had sat in the swing talking with them. Now it surprised me to learn that their youngest of seven children was a teenager. As he exited the kitchen's back door, I was thankful Mother could not see us from her kitchen window. The way he smiled at me made me nervous, and he asked the question again. "Are you going to the circus?"

I hedged for a second and made sure we were far up the street before I answered, "Yes."

I could not think as he continued. "My name is Ray, and I am on the football team with your brother. Do you want to go to the circus with me?"

I began, "Oh no! I'm meeting a friend."

He laughed. "Okay, I will just walk up the street with you."

By the time Ray and I got to Mercer Street, Maggie had almost given up on me. I introduced her to my new neighbor. He asked, "Is it all right if I tag along with you and Ivy?" She had already replied *yes* before she saw my head shaking *no*.

We had our own three-ring circus walking toward the high school football field as the witty upperclassman entertained us. When we started home, Ray suggested, "Let's go to the drugstore and have something cold to drink." Ray ordered three cherry Cokes and three packs of Nabs and handed the clerk a $5 bill for the 31¢ purchase. Maggie and I looked at each other! We had never seen a student with that big of a bill.

Afterward, Ray and I left Maggie where we had met her; and when we got to the side of his house, I figured the only way to get out of this without Mother seeing me from her kitchen window was to insist on going in his back door to speak to his parents. Once inside, I said, "Oh, I just remembered something I have to do. See you later." I ran out the back door, around the corner, and straight into my house.

As I started up the steps, Mother called from the kitchen. "Why were you running?"

The next morning, as I washed the breakfast dishes, Ray was waiting on the corner to walk me to Nob School on his way to high school. I went upstairs to finish dressing; I knew I could outwait him because he had farther to walk. I outwaited him mornings and lunchtimes. However, late Wednesday afternoon, I walked by his house on my way home from a GA meeting, and I heard him say, "Hey, where have you been? I haven't seen you around."

I lied, "I have been busy with graduation."

He asked, "Will you be at Nan's neighborhood party on Saturday night?"

I lied, "Sure! I have to run, but I will see you there."

The springtime party was a celebration of graduation and Nan's birthday. The gang from the ball field and my siblings would be there. At the last minute, I begged Mother to let me go.

When I arrived, Ray was waiting for me! Before everyone had shown up, Ray began, "I want to play pleased or displeased."

Nan, a fun-loving girl, replied, "Okay, Ray, are you pleased or displeased?"

He shouted, "I am displeased."

Nan shouted back, "Okay, what will it take to please you?"

He stood up, pointed at me, and shouted, "I want to walk around the house and kiss Ivy at every corner." Red-faced and angry, I refused to go.

Nan laughed. "Okay, Ivy, go with Ray."

I repeated, "No."

The group began chanting, "You have to play fair."

I realized that, by refusing, I caused more commotion. I stood up, Ray took my hand, and we walked down the steps. Indeed, he kissed me at each corner. Those four long kisses were overwhelming! We walked back up the porch, and he wanted to sit in the swing instead of going back in the house. Before he had completely sat down, his arms went around me, and his lips were on mine.

The years of abuse taught me not only that I did not have the right to protect my body but also that I did not have a right to hurt anyone's feelings by saying *no* if they made me feel uncomfortable. It was a paradox that, by eighth grade, I had spent years in my parents' bedroom, yet I was innocent of the sexual sensation, much less the sexual act. I only had girlish dreams that one day Prince Charming would come along and save me, and we would live happily ever afterward, just as it happened to Cinderella.

To my horror, I heard the group in the living room trying to talk all at once. "Ray kissed Ivy at every corner of the house, and now they are kissing on the front porch."

I knew my brothers had arrived by way of the kitchen door when I heard John instruct Steve, "Go home and tell Mother." I waited! When

Steve returned, he never said a word to me. I finally had the fortitude to slip away home after another evening of being out of control of my life. Thankfully, no one in the family ever mentioned my night of kissing a boy in public.

On graduation night from eighth grade at Nob School, I proudly walked up the street in a powder blue dress with big puffy sleeves. After weeks of rehearsing marching down the aisle to the school band playing "Pomp and Circumstance," the actual ceremony finally arrived.

When my two brothers graduated, Mother took a whole roll of film of them in cap and gown. However, the night of my graduation, I left home disappointed that she had only taken one picture of me, and no family member showed up to see me graduate.

After the ceremony, the custodian sealed the building, and only the members of the graduation class were allowed to attend the big party in the gymnasium. Halfway through the celebration, Brut told me that the custodian told him that two guys, Seth and Ray, were waiting out on the front steps to walk me home. The one night I did not have to hurry home, I wanted to go home. I asked the boy whose glasses I had broken if he would get the custodian to let us out the back door. Brut walked me home and returned to the party.

A few mornings later, I entered the kitchen; and for the first time, Mother mentioned Ray. "I see you have lost your boyfriend to Sally." I walked to the kitchen window to see what she referred to. Ray had hung the porch swing from a large tree in his front yard, and there he and my best friend in the neighborhood, Sally, sat kissing.

What made me angry the most was Mother never encouraged me with nice boys. She had teased me about getting involved with poor, helpless men who circulated around town with mental or alcohol problems. Because the elder children in the area tormented these men unmercifully, Uncle Bob and I felt sorry for them and took the time to talk to them.

One such evening, I came out of a neighbor's house, and one of these fellows happened to be passing by. I felt sorry for the disturbed man of short stature. I returned his greeting, and he began a long discussion concerning the Korean conflict, the hot weather, and our town. I finally sat down on the grassy area between the sidewalk and the road and listened to him.

When I entered the house, I learned that Mother and Daddy had been watching us from their bedroom window. Mother hurried down the steps. Looking proud, she instructed me, "Now there is a nice guy, and I think you will marry him."

I cried and said, "Why would you want me to marry a man who is not capable of working or supporting a family?"

For the hundredth time in my short life, she repeated, "Only one girl will make me proud, and that will be Susie."

The weather and the lack of communication had an adverse effect on the war raging in Korea. The spring rains caused flooding, and the mud kept the soldiers from fighting. When the Communists decided to end the war, they claimed themselves the winners and began attacking the south up to the time of the signing of the armistice.

By the time the war news ended, the television had become a habit, if not an addiction, in most American homes. We had watched clips of World War II at the movie house; now the Korean conflict played out in our living rooms. The Korean conflict lasted just over three years, and I missed the celebration of the end of the war in my hometown because Granddad Ooking sent me back to the GA camp for the second year in a row.

When I arrived at the Cedars, to my disappointment, I found that Nancy had not come back to be a counselor. I had vowed to become queen and repeat the thirteenth chapter of 1 Corinthians at my coronation service, and I wanted her to prepare me. The last night of camp, I would be crowned queen in a candlelight service, but I would repeat the ceremony before my church family when I returned home.

My granddad wanted me to have the best of white dresses for the ceremony at the camp. After all the years of conflict with Mother over the outfits that she ordered from Sears, she shook my world of fashion by the dress she purchased at the Mademoiselle shop in town. She purchased a replica of a dress worn by Doris Day in a movie. The white dotted Swiss dress had a circular skirt, little green buttons, and a green ribbon for the sash. For the first time in my life, I truly felt like a queen in that movie star's dress, quoting my chapter from the Bible.

Arriving back home, I could not wait to show off my gorgeous Doris Day dress at church. I jumped out of bed earlier than usual on Sunday morning, unpacked the dress, and plugged in the iron to press out every wrinkle. With the skirt hanging on the end of the ironing board, I sat the hot iron on the skirt. When I picked up the iron, there was a hole the size and shape of the iron on the skirt fabric. With tears streaming down my cheeks, I grabbed the dress and ran upstairs before Mother got out of bed. I knew I had to wear the dress to church so Granddad Ooking could see me in it. I practiced folding that section of the circular skirt in such a way that the hole would not show. I had lost my confidence and did not prance around in my new dress, and the only comments I received when I arrived at church were "Why are you holding the skirt of your dress in such a strange manner?" That was the beginning and end of my confidence in the fashion world.

The fashion world brought back the styles that were popular in the late 1930s when I entered high school. The Sears, Roebuck & Co. catalog pictured bobby socks, saddle oxfords, fifty-yard crinolines, full skirts, seamless nylons, and ballerina flats. I learned very fast that the small high school of over nine hundred students had a very definite set of standards for one to be included in the elite crowd.

I did not live on the right side of Main Street, although my grandparents did. Moreover, Mother wouldn't agree to let me wear the latest style, which included the crinoline under a full skirt. Mother refused to order the stylish clothing for my first year of high school. She informed me, "You are too fat to wear full crinolines and full skirts."

I hated the lectures that followed when the Sears packages finally arrived. Daddy talked fifteen minutes on the importance of wearing good heavy shoes and the proper way of taking care of them. As we got older, Mother continued giving her speech: "I work my fingers to the bone cleaning, washing, ironing, and cooking. And by the time I buy your clothes, I cannot afford a thing for myself."

The first morning of my freshman year, I hurried to finish the house chores because I had three blocks farther to run to high school. By ninth grade, I had gotten used to my sweaty odor as I slipped into a new straight skirt, pullover sweater, neck scarf, bobby socks, and saddle oxfords. I ran past Nob School, where I had spent the last five years. As eighth graders, the teachers had warned our class, "When you get to high school, you will go from top dog to lowly freshmen."

I entered a large building with hundreds of students running in every direction. I felt as if I were in a whirlwind as I ran in circles, trying to find my homeroom before the tardy bell rang. As fate would have it, the first person I encountered in the midst of the confusion was my former tomboy best friend from third grade, who had held me down in the snow so Donald could kiss me. Now over five years later, I stood in the hall of the high school looking at a beautiful, delicate, and graceful young lady with long flowing blond hair instead of her pigtails.

To add to the shock of her transformation, my former best friend from Nob School, Ashley, had developed into an even more gorgeous young lady. My two former best friends had connected in high school, and every time I saw the two friends together, I wished that they would include me. However, even with the honor of being the only freshman cheerleader on the high school squad, Ashley found the time to join me as a guard on the freshman girls' basketball team.

When it came to getting my wish for the first year of high school, I bit off more than I could chew in Mr. Shot's algebra class. He really cared about me enough to threaten to stop by the building supply shop and talk to my granddaddy if I did not shape up. I wanted to please him, but I did not know how to tell him that he entered my life too late. I also had him for homeroom, and he campaigned for my election as student council representative. A few times, he took me in the hall and explained, "Ivy, you have such potential, and I want to make something out of you. Why don't you cooperate and do better in your classwork?"

I did not know how to verbalize that I had to help with breakfast, make seven beds, clean floors, and wash dishes before getting ready for school every morning. Once I got to school, I felt intimidated by being late, tired, and dirty and could not comprehend subject matters.

During my first year of high school, many changes had taken place in our home. First, Dad and Granddad Ooking disagreed on Granddad retiring and turning the business over to Dad because he was not dependable. Therefore, Dad went back to the union, which he had joined during their argument during World War II, and signed up for an electrical job in Ohio.

Toward the end of my freshman year, Uncle Bob finally had to reveal where he had been going on his mysterious weekends for the last seven years. He and Pat had to announce their secret marriage because they were expecting a baby in late summer, and they moved into their new home. The third person leaving the home for me was the most painful. As soon as John graduated from high school, he left for college.

The morning John drove off in Granddad Ooking's old 1942 car to college, I went into Uncle Bob and his bedroom, lay on John's twin bed in the empty room, and began crying loudly. I felt weak from crying when I heard footsteps and looked up, and there stood John! He had forgotten something! He begged, "Don't cry. That makes it more difficult to leave!"

Even with the pressure of dodging Daddy whenever I walked through the house, it surprised me how cold and empty the house became without him to occupy Mother's time. I also realized that, in some ways, he had tried to protect me. I thought of the many times he confronted Mother and demanded Susie take turns in helping with the dishes. Of course, Mother would scream in defense of her daughter. Their war raged on and on, but nothing had ever changed for me. I could not understand why Susie never seemed happy since she was free from chores, her mother defended her, and she even slept with Mother since Daddy left.

The worst situation happened one night as my brother John stood at my parents' bedroom door, carrying on a debate with Daddy. I had already gone to bed. While Daddy went into a long discussion, my brother walked into my room, pulled the covers down, and stuck his finger in my vagina. Oh, the horrifying pain! I knew that if I screamed, my parents would not believe what my brother had just done to me. Afterward, as smooth as silk, my brother walked back to the door just in time to give his side of the debate to Dad. When the discussion ended, he went to his room. I went to the bathroom and found blood on my clothes and no one to defend me.

However, after the year of family separations, good news came the first month of summer vacation. Mother sent for her mama to come and keep house while she visited Daddy in Ohio. It had been six years since we moved in our new home. By the time my parents turned the corner on the avenue heading to Ohio, I was out the door.

Unfortunately, with my newfound freedom, I didn't find one person at the ball field. Therefore, I visited my girl friend Jean, who lived in the next block, as she babysat her sister for her working mother. Other times, I talked Nan and her sister, Babes, into coming to the ball field to play Indian ball with Susie and me.

In playing Indian ball, one person would throw the ball into the air and hit it into the outfield. From the point where a fielder took possession of the ball, he would roll it toward home plate and try to hit the bat lying crosswise. If the fielder succeeded, he became the next batter.

One afternoon, as I ran toward home plate screaming for joy because I had hit the bat, a truckload of furniture with a teenage boy sitting on the back drove by. Nan and I stopped the game, jumped up on the sidewalk, and saw the truck stop by the first house on the left in the next block.

The next afternoon, Nan and I used the excuse of needing ballplayers to knock on the door of our new neighbors. We knocked on the front door and a nice woman answered, and hesitantly, I asked, "Do you have a boy or—I mean, any children who would like to play ball?"

The woman smiled and said, "My son isn't home, and my little girl is only four years old." We took off running and laughing.

Nan's backyard backed up to the new family's backyard. The next day, she suggested, "We might be able to meet the guy if we offer to cut the tall weeds in their backyard."

This time, a man came to the door, and I asked him, "Would you like us to cut the weeds in your backyard?"

He replied, "Well, the weeds sure need cutting, but do you think you can cut tall ones?"

We shouted, "Yes, yes!"

Nan, Babes, and I stood in grass and weeds that came to our waists as we began using my friend's sickle and clippers. Two hours later, exhausted from cutting, chopping, and twisting weeds, we had not made a dent in the project, nor had we seen the teenage boy. Finally, the man came outside, handed us $2, and said, "Thank you for the hard work. I'll finish the rest." To add to the confusion, every time we tried to find out the family's name, we got a different name.

Sunday at church, I told Jill about the two funny incidents of trying to meet the new guy in the neighborhood and that he was more like a phantom than a human being. She laughed and volunteered, "I will have a wiener roast and invite him, and Mother can find out about the family since his mother is a nurse also."

Later, Jill told me that her mother, Eliz, had learned that my new heartthrob's name was Ed and that he lived with his stepfather and mother, Richard and Pam. The reason we could not find his telephone number with the operator was that the family had not one last name listed but three—Ed's, his stepfather's, and his grandma's, who lived with them. Finally, Jill got Ed's telephone number from the operator and invited him to the wiener roast, along with his friends, to make sure he would attend.

Show up he did! He and a group of his fellow high school dance band members arrived in a rowdy mood. For the first time, I stood close to him, and I still felt attracted to him. However, the only awareness he had shown toward me was by throwing a long sharp fork, which we used to roast wieners, and it stuck in the ground between my feet. When he began running, I pulled the instrument out of the ground and chased after him. When he started toward the dark alley, I turned and went back to the crowd.

Ed and his friends left for the rec center a few blocks from Jill's home. When Eliz gave Jill permission to go to the high school hangout with the other girls, I had to make a choice to either go with them or go home. Unquestionably, my parents had forbidden me to go to the rec center since it opened, and I had never stepped foot in it. Jill convinced me that we had gone through too much trouble to meet Ed for me to walk away now. She also figured that since Ed and I lived so close to each other, we could walk home together. I entered the forbidden teenage hangout, hanging on to Jill's coattail and whispering to her, "Do not leave me alone."

When I entered the rec center, I entered a new world that I did not know existed. I did not know how to become part of the crowd with the loud music from the jukebox and the rowdy crowd dancing to the blaring music. I felt awkward and uncomfortable, and I wanted to get home. I tried to persuade my good friend to ask Ed to walk home with me, and she instructed, "It's too early. Wait until the crowd begins breaking up." One thing was for sure: I did not want to get to know Ed badly enough to wait until later. I went out into the crisp night air alone and walked home with the moon watching over me.

The next afternoon, Mama walked around the area, teaching me the art of picking her favorite growing, wild creasy greens. After a dinner of soul food, she told me to run along and play with my friends. As usual, no one came to the ball field these days. The big idea hit me— why not visit my friend Jean, who lived only two houses past Ed's?

With an ulterior motive, I suggested to Jean that we sit in her porch swing and talk. Just at dusk, while we were swinging and chatting, Bud came out of his house straight across the street from Ed's house. I called out for him to come over. What I did not know at the time was that I had upset Jean because she had been avoiding Bud, who had a crush on her.

To break the strain between the two, I took great liberties in quizzing Bud about the new boy in the neighborhood. He knew Ed well: "Ed will be a senior in high school, is a photographer of the yearbook, plays in the school orchestra, is president of the model aircraft club, and loves motorcycles."

Now that the night had gotten darker, I stood to go home when a car pulled in front of the new family's house, and Ed got out. I pinched Bud's arm and whispered, "Please, please call him over here."

He shouted, "Hey, Ed, there is a girl over here who wants to meet you."

I jumped up and grabbed Bud's mouth when I heard Ed say, "Have you been to any wiener roasts lately?"

There he stood in dress slacks, sports shirt, and sports coat. He smiled at me, and I replied, "No."

Bud said, "I am supposed to be in the yard digging worms if I want Daddy to take me fishing in the morning." He looked at Jean. "Have you ever dug for worms?"

She made a face and said, "No."

Ed suggested, "Let's take the girls digging for worms."

Once in the backyard, Bud began pulling the longest, fattest, and juiciest night crawlers from the freshly dug hole, and Jean and I felt sick. Ed held his fist in front of me and announced, "I found a dime."

I walked away from him, thinking that he must have a worm, and he challenged, "I dare you to open my hand." In my almost sixteen-year-old mind, I dreamed of meeting Prince Charming, getting married, having two children and a little white house with a white picket fence, and living happily ever after. Therefore, I did not know what drew me to Ed. We were about the same size and totally opposites of my dream couple.

Jean and I agreed that we had to get home before we got in trouble for being out too late. I walked across the street with Ed, and he invited me to sit in the swing on his front porch. We settled into the swing as I asked, "Is your family home?"

He shared, "My great-grandmother died, and she is still at the funeral home."

"Is that why you are dressed up?"

"Yes. I could only stand so much of death, and I went out with my friends."

The summer night air had become chilly, and I could not believe when the teenager took off his sports coat and wrapped it around my shoulders. That was when I smelled his breath and asked, "Have you been drinking alcohol?"

He laughed. "Yes, I had a couple of beers with the guys."

Vulnerable, uneducated, and ignorant of human nature, I faced my first experience of dealing with the social and moral issues in life. Until that moment, I did not know that I had any convictions until I heard myself saying, "Don't you think drinking will ruin your life?"

He replied, "I just had a couple of beers."

I could not understand why I felt comfortable looking into his pleasant smile, white teeth, high cheekbones, black hair, and eyes that stood out even in the dark night with his suntan that made his skin even darker. Somewhere deep in my being, I thought he looked like the man who had held me on his lap and told me that I would always be his little girl. I continued. "Don't you know alcohol splits up families?" He laughed and reached his left arm around my shoulder, and I asked, "Don't you even care what God thinks?"

Boy, did I hit a nerve, and the monologue now became a dialogue when he replied, "I don't believe there is a god."

There had been times when Steve tried to upset me in front of Mother by saying, "Why should you go to church when there isn't a god?" However, this first blow from Ed had me laboring and straining for a defense of my god who shielded me in my lonely pilgrimage on this earth.

The storm grew worse when he interrupted. "Tell me, if there is a god, why did he let my parents divorce when I was two years old and I never got to grow up with my daddy or fly in his airplane? After the divorce, why did I lose my mother when she went back to nurse training and left me with her parents? Every time she came home, I pleaded with her not to go back to school. When I was four years old, I lay in the backseat of the car crying for her not to get on the train and leave me. One day as I cried, suddenly, I decided that I would never cry or let anyone hurt me again. Nevertheless, my grandfather became my best friend, taught me to fish, shoot a gun, and love nature. When I was in eighth grade, he had a heart attack. I watched him die, and I feel guilty and hurt that I could not save him."

Death was somber but never so much as at that moment. I had never had anyone close to me die. All I knew about death were the neighborhood social wakes I had attended when I was in grade school. I had no answers! I saw for the first time that I could not judge people because I did not know what burdens they carried. I would be sixteen years old in a couple of months, and all I could say was "I am sorry! I do not understand, but I do know there is a god, and I trust God."

At that moment, I reached out, took his hand in mine, and told him that I had to get home. We walked out onto the sidewalk in silence. I felt fear when I did not see a light on in our two-story house, and I quietly opened the front door. Ed took his jacket from my shoulders, kissed me, grabbed a comic book off a lawn chair, and ran.

I had never had an adult counsel me along life's pathways. I shared my dreams with my girl friends, and they did not have life's experiences to warn me of getting involved in unhealthy relationships. This was especially true if that person came from a well-known family in the community that most people approved of. Ed's mother worked as a supervisor of the hospital, and to know her was to love her. His stepfather's family had earned respect in the community by producing great teachers. Therefore, with the approval of my girl friend's families, I dated Ed.

Oh, how embarrassing it was the day I walked toward Jean's house and got the shock of my life. In the driveway, Ed, his friend, and his father were working on an old motorbike. I tried to sneak by when Ed shouted, "Hey, wait a minute." He walked to the sidewalk and took hold of my hand in broad daylight. Finally, I got enough presence of mind to make up a reason why I had to hurry on to Jean's house so he would let go of my hand.

Later, Ed told me how he had traded antique photograph equipment for the motorbike. He had overhauled the engine, but it was still hard to start. Many times, he tried jump-starting it by pushing it back and forth through the back alley from his house, across the intersection, and past the back of my house. His mechanical abilities impressed me.

I avoided Ed the day Dad and Mother were due home from Ohio because I knew it would be trouble if they saw me with a boy. Jake, our six-foot-four-inch all-star basketball-playing cousin, came to visit that evening as we waited for our parents' return.

Before leaving the building supply business, Daddy had upgraded the ten-inch television to a fourteen-inch screen. By experimenting, he learned the reception came in better on the enclosed back porch than in the back bedroom. He built a shelf over the laundry tub for the television set. Mother hung curtains at the row of windows and put a couch at the far end, and it became a cozy room for the warm weather.

However, the popularity of television had replaced the ball field, front porches, and bike riding. I had spent years trying to get out of the house, and now everyone voluntarily stayed inside. The good news about television was that it had taken a lot of attention off me and to Milton Berle's vaudeville routines. How I loved to listen to Mother and Steve laugh as they repeated many of Berle's one-liners.

This night, Jake joined us on the back porch; and in the midst of watching *Your Show of Shows* with Sid Caesar and Imogene Coca, Steve appeared in the kitchen doorway and announced, "Ivy, someone is in the living room to see you."

Excitedly, I jumped up off the couch and ran into the horror of my life. There stood the boyfriend in our house. *Mother will kill me.* Panicked, I rudely asked, "What are you doing here?"

Calmly, Ed answered as he walked toward the couch and sat down, "I could not find a telephone number for you, you were not at your friend's house, and I wanted to see you."

I followed as I told him, "We do not have a telephone, and we are busy preparing for our parents to come home tonight." I tried to think! I have never had a boy in the house! Would my parents come home earlier than expected? My brothers would tell on me! To add to my impossible situation, I saw Mama's white hair as she peeped around the archway between the living room and dining room, and I could hear the others whispering and giggling. Then utterly confused, Susie, her friend Betty, Jake, and Steve walked through and went into the back bedroom.

Steve knew Ed was in the high school orchestra, and the members did not like country music. Therefore, from the back bedroom, "Your Cheatin' Heart" blasted through the house from a country radio station. Suddenly, Susie and Betty appeared, beating on metal wastebaskets, followed by Steve blowing his baritone and my cousin blowing the antique trombone. They marched right in front of us, up the steps, through the hall, back down, and through the living room, dining room, and kitchen, laughing hysterically. I kept talking as if nothing out of the ordinary was happening and never acknowledged the strange behavior.

However, it did convince Ed that he should leave. I stood in the foyer talking to him with my hands behind my back when Susie opened the French doors and said, "It is bedtime," putting a clock in my hand.

I stepped backward, threw our first electric clock at her, and heard glass breaking as she shouted, "Oh, you broke our new clock!"

To my surprise, Ed asked, "When can I see you again?"

I managed to say, "I have to wait and see what my parents have planned."

Once I shut the front door, I ran up the steps crying, and my brother and sister called after me. "Just you wait until Mother gets home. We will tell her you had a boy in the house."

Later that night, I woke to hear commotion at the front door and Susie saying, "And Ivy had a boy in the house! She broke the face off the new clock!"

Mother replied, "We have had a long day! We can talk about Dumb Ivy tomorrow."

The next day, I helped Mother with Dad's laundry before his return trip to work on Sunday. I watched as Ed kept pushing his bike up and down the alley, but I would not go out to hang clothes on the line when he was at my end of the alley.

That evening, Mother dropped a bombshell. "Ivy and Steve are going to Ohio with Daddy in the morning. In a couple of weeks, Susie and I will arrive by bus for the rest of the summer." I could not get out of the house to tell Ed that I would be leaving. The next morning, I convinced Steve to sit in the front seat with Daddy, and I climbed in the backseat to grieve over the fact that I had not told any of my friends I would be gone for the rest of the summer.

Around midafternoon, we arrived in Waverly, Ohio, where Daddy introduced us to his twenty-four-foot trailer in the Brooklyn Acres trailer park, a large laundry facility, and the general store. Steve and I made twin beds from the two chairs in the living room, and Daddy slept in the three-quarter bed in the little bedroom.

The next morning, he left for work in the Piketon area, where he worked as an electrician in the construction of a uranium plant. Long after he had left, a woman knocked on the door and jarred us out of bed. She introduced herself as Mrs. Adkins and said that she had promised Daddy that she would keep an eye on us, and she invited us to her beautiful large trailer next door for breakfast.

After a delicious breakfast, Steve and I walked to the other end of the park to check out the Laundromat and followed the path to the grocery store to purchase items for Daddy's dinner. I saw stationery and stamps and decided to write Ed. "This is the first time I ever left town for the summer, and I had no way of getting word to you."

Within a week, I had an answer. He mailed me a picture of himself with at least a three-inch-high crew cut, and I tore it to pieces and threw it in the drain opening, where I knew Dad would not find it. He wrote a very interesting letter (if you were his mother): "My great-uncle came back from Florida with a pet baby alligator. In addition, I wish you could see the souvenirs he brought us from the Philippines. When will you be home? I miss you."

I could not answer his letter because, by the time I received his reply, I knew Mother and Susie would have arrived. I buried my sorrow of leaving Ed by attending a new ministry, which a pastor had started in a movie theater. I always felt at home in church on Sundays, and I played on the youth's ball team and attended all the church's summer outings.

Two wonderful, carefree weeks passed without difficulties until Dad pulled up in front of the trailer and let Mother and Susie out of the car. I ran from preparing Dad's dinner to welcome them and hardly recognized Susie! She no longer looked like a tomboy. In a short length of time, she had gotten taller and slimmer. I heard Mother inform Dad, "Just look, Susie became a young woman this summer. I had to buy her all new clothes, and she got a new hairstyle."

Those words cut deeply into my heart. I had a great desire to be slim, pretty, and a young woman with a new hairstyle like my sister. I had run around the trailer park for two weeks in the same two-piece short shorts and halter set, which Mother had a neighbor make for me. Susie and I could have been good friends and shared our years growing up together if Mother had left us alone.

It had just been a year before when Susie told me, "I am going to dry the dishes because I feel guilty for not helping." There seemed to be an instant bond between us. While I washed, she dried.

I began sharing a true story about a neighbor family. "The parents received a thirty-day notice to vacate the rental house. With only days left, they had not found one. The family prayed to find a house one night. The next day, a man called and offered to rent them one."

Susie and I had never heard of an answered prayer. She replied, "Really!"

At that moment, Mother jumped around the corner, laughing so hard she could hardly say, "Poor Dumb Ivy."

Mother took Susie by the shoulder and instructed, "Put that dish towel down, go outside to play, and let Dumb Ivy do the dishes alone."

Because I stayed in trouble with Mother, Susie decided to go the opposite direction from the things I did. She and her friend began skipping Sunday school and using their offerings for cigarettes and

Cokes and never once got in trouble. Through the years of conflict, a definite separation had developed in our standards and morals.

Now that separation would continue back in the hot trailer in Ohio. I could never have believed that Mother could assign me enough chores in that small trailer to keep me separated from her and Susie.

Because of the heat, Daddy installed a canvas awning on the front of the trailer so we could sit outside. Mother and Susie sat under the awning discussing which words fit into the crossword puzzles while I scrubbed and waxed every inch of the trailer's paneling and appliances. By midafternoon, when it was just too hot to be in the trailer, Mother either sent me to the Laundromat or humiliated me by making me stand under the awning ironing.

After the first part of a scorching August, it came time to return to our hometown to prepare for school. For me, Dad could not drive fast enough to get home. Since Mama kept our house clean, the next morning, I volunteered to mow the lawn. I pushed and pushed the lawn mower in the high grass until I nearly passed out from the heat before slipping off to Jean's house.

However, I just got to Ed's house when he appeared and shouted, "I saw your dad's car, and I've been looking for you. I want you to see that I traded my nonrunning motor scooter for a nonworking motorbike." I cut the visit short and stressed the fact that Uncle Bob and Pat were expecting their first baby any day and that I would not be able to see him for a while.

Early the next morning, Uncle Bob stopped by the house to ask his sister if she would go to the hospital to stay with Pat. Since we did not have a telephone, Mother could not get word to us about how things were going. To keep from worrying, Mama kept busy in the kitchen. Susie and I were on the back porch watching Pinky Lee on television when my grandmother announced, "Ivy, you have company."

Instantly, Ed appeared from behind her, walked out on the porch, and sat beside me on the couch. The room began spinning, and I heard him say, "I haven't seen you out today." I kept staring at the television set, and he continued. "Are you upset with me?"

I managed to get "no" out of my mouth before I lied, "We are worried about my aunt who is in labor at the hospital."

The timing could not have been worse. Within half an hour, Mother appeared in the kitchen and announced to her mother, "Your son has a fine, healthy son. They named him Ed."

She walked out on the porch and stared at me, and I stammered, "Mother, I would like for you to meet my friend, Ed—"

Before I could finish the introduction, she smiled and began a friendly chat. "I've been at the hospital all day with my sister-in-law who just had a baby boy. Would you like some of these fried apple pies my mother made?" Ed assured her that he would love one.

While they were interacting, I wondered why she befriended him. Finally, I could not stand the pressure any longer. I suggested to Ed, "Mother has had a hard day. Let's call it an evening."

After he left, all Mother had to say was "You are not to sit on the dark porch with a boy wearing those short shorts."

A couple of nights later, the fearless Ed knocked on the door just as Mother and Steve had been trying to adjust the television reception. Ed took over the fine-tuning and adjustments of our antenna like a professional. When Ed got a better picture than even Daddy ever did, we were all impressed with him.

Once we were alone, he told me, "You should see my room since I am an amateur radio enthusiast with a novice license. Mother refuses to clean the wall-to-wall electronic junk."

All I knew was to ask, "What is a novice license?"

He told me, "A man by the name of Samuel Morse invented the telegraph and assigned every letter in the alphabet a signal, like the man in the western movies clicking dots and dashes on a key."

On August 30, 1954, my sixteenth birthday, I could not believe the surprise waiting for me at the front door. Ed handed me two wrapped presents with a large envelope. Before he left, I unwrapped them and discovered an unusual wallet covered in a white plastic substance resembling pearls and a long pin lined with pearls like many girls wore at the neck of their blouses. His mother had made a large heart-shaped cookie, and on it she printed, "Happy birthday, Dot."

It would take a guy with Ed's fortitude to break down the invisible barriers that held me prisoner in my home. He persisted against my warnings! The one battle Mother did win, at the beginning of my sophomore year, was to put a stop to him sitting in the living room while waiting until I got my chores finished to walk me to school. She demanded, "Tell Ed if he wants to walk to school with you, he can wait at the corner," and he did.

Mr. Shot, on the other hand, made no bones about his disapproval of the upperclassman the day Ed walked me to my homeroom. My favorite teacher assured me, "You are too young to get involved with a senior," and he gave me good advice that I wished for myself: "Wait until you get to college and find an educated young man."

Ed had not done any better in Mr. Shot's algebra class than I did. However, he did well in geometry, which I now struggled with in my second year of high school. The best part of going to geometry class was when Ed passed me notes written in Morse code. Dan, who sat behind me in class, would try to grab them from me. Later in the year, Dan succeeded in snatching a note, and I laughed. "Ha, try to read it."

He laughed. "Ha, I have a copy of the Morse code from the library."

To add to the new changes that Ed brought into my life, he forced another issue with Mother, which I feared would put me back in my parents' bedroom. Ed came to the house and invited me to a movie. I replied, "There is no way Mother will let me go with a boy."

He insisted, "Either you ask her or I will."

After pleading with him to leave, I gave in and walked to the kitchen where I asked, "Mother, may I go to the movies with Ed tonight?"

She started, "No, I don't—"

Steve interrupted, "Let her go."

After Ed left, I ran up the steps and put on my new Sears skirt when I heard Mother shout, "Susie, you get ready and go with them."

Susie began crying, "I do not want to go with them."

Steve continued his defense for my case. "What is wrong with them walking up the street to a movie?"

Finally, I thought Mother gave up with her two teenagers on my side. Nevertheless, just before the lights went down low in the theater, I saw Steve and Susie walking down the aisle on the other side of the movie house. At the same time, the beautiful, fresh, clean Terri dressed in the latest style, on the arm of the most popular boy in town, passed by us; and I scrunched down in my seat. I did not want her to see me in my cheap outfit and with a guy who had the reputation of being a beer drinker.

Usually after the movie, the teenagers went to one of the two drugstores in town for Cokes and crackers. However, after the movie, Ed walked me to a nearby restaurant for a milk shake. For the first time in my life, I felt like a grown-up sitting in a booth, looking across the table at a young man who gave me his full attention, which I badly needed.

The evening ended when I entered the house. Mother had been trying to get Steve to go look for me, and she screamed, "When the movie lets out, you are to be in this house in fifteen minutes."

The next Thursday, carrying my two eggs, I walked to the church sunrise Thanksgiving breakfast. Once I returned home, I had to do the semiannual job of scrubbing the cooking stove. Down on my knees, with my arms in the oven, I heard Ed speak. "I want to invite you to Thanksgiving dinner at my house later today."

I jumped up with black grease to my elbows and insisted that Mother would not let me go. He only said, "You ask your mother, or I will."

I walked to the living room with Ed as my protector to ask permission, and Mother just replied, "Only if you get that stove clean."

When Ed returned, I had dressed in another one of the new Sears outfits, and we walked out the block to his house. The shock of my life came when we entered his house, and it looked like Christmastime. His family and relatives gathered around the extended table of a complete turkey dinner, greeting me as if I was someone important.

I took the excitement back home and tried to describe the celebration to my siblings. They would not believe me until Mother confirmed, "Yes, some people have Thanksgiving feasts like our Christmas feast."

For the next month, Ed and I went to the movie every weekend and to church on Sunday. The schedule worked peacefully until Christmas Eve and the high school Christmas dance became an issue. I refused to approach Mother for permission, and my "knight in shining armor" challenged her hold on me once more. Because of his bravery, I attended his family festivities from nine to midnight on Christmas Eve and felt important taking home Jewel Tea Christmas gifts of a comb set, scarf, gloves, perfume, and jewelry. After a great Christmas, I got out my year-old formal gown to prepare for the 1954 Christmas dance.

The Christmas before, I had asked for an evening gown so I could go to the formal with my freshman friends. Mother had told me, "You know we can't afford to buy you an expensive dress."

However, just days before that Christmas—I could not recall why I was home alone—I went snooping for Christmas presents and saw a large box under my parents' bed. I had the audacity to open it. In hindsight, I was amazed at the nerve not only to open the gigantic box but also to put on the ballerina-length formal gown. Next, I opened a shoebox and put on the blue pumps. Then I paraded up and down the hallway as if it was a Paris runway and practiced walking in high heels.

Those were the times when I had never seen Scotch tape in our house. Somehow, I slid the large gown box back in the wrapping paper by sticking new Christmas seals to hold it together. Not only had I ruined my Christmas surprise but I also had nowhere to wear that frock that year.

Now a year later, I nervously walked the floor in the beautiful dress and waited for Ed to arrive. He surprised me with a corsage, which he pinned on my gown. When we started out the door, Mother dampened our spirits by demanding, "Ivy, you have to be in this house at intermission, midnight."

As we walked out the sidewalk toward Ed's home for his parents to take pictures of us and wait for the couple we were double-dating with, Ed said, "Let's go back and tell your mother we are going to stay at the dance until it is over, two in the morning." I convinced him that she might make me stay home.

Ed's grandmother put her mink jacket around my shoulders and insisted that I go to the formal in style, which added a special touch to the special evening.

When I entered my first ballroom dance, I hardly recognized the girls I saw daily in the halls of high school as they flowed around the circular room in beautiful flowing gowns. Ed would not allow me to take my position as a wallflower. He put his arms around me and waltzed me to the middle of the floor. My friends had taught me to

jitterbug in gym class, and Ed and I laughed as he really cut a rug to
Bill Haley and His Comets' "Rock around the Clock."

At intermission, Ed took me home as promised. He and the rest
of my friends continued with the festivities until two. The dance had
been fun, but I did not feel as comfortable with the dressed-up crowd
as I did at church or with Ed and his family.

I did not understand how a teenager who was brave enough to
begin liberating me from bondage would not have the nerve to ask me
if I would go steady with him. He seemed mature by putting his sports
coat around my shoulder, kissing my hand when parting, and crashing
our home to give me a social life. However, a few weeks after taking
me to the Christmas dance, Ed blurted out, "The guys are betting 50¢
that you will not go steady with me."

I hurt him as I answered, "If you are asking me to win a bet, the
answer is no!" He got up and walked out the front door. I ran to my
bedroom, sat on the foot of my bed, and watched him plow through the
snow that was almost to his knees. My heart ached when I saw him go
out of sight toward town and not to his home.

I watched for him to appear at the corner the next morning to
walk me to school, but he never did. I looked for him between classes
without any luck. The pain in the core of my being produced tears in
my eyes all morning.

Thankfully, the basketball team had scheduled a game against
the teachers for the afternoon. I sat in the bleachers crying until I saw
flashbulbs flashing from the balcony. I knew he had come to fulfill his
duty as the yearbook's photographer. I ran onto the floor, looked up,
and saw his substitute. I cried myself to sleep that night and walked
to school by myself again the next morning.

At lunchtime, I walked in the middle of the road to stay out of the
line of snowball battles. When one hit me in the middle of my back, I
picked up a handful of snow and turned to throw it. My heart skipped
a beat when I saw Ed. I slowed my speed, but he never caught up with
me. By the time I had the lunch dishes done, I saw him standing at the
corner.

We walked in silence a few minutes before he shocked me by
telling me where he had been. "I took a bottle of liquor, went to Doug's
pond, and ice-skated until late last night." It was all I could do to keep

my opinion to myself before he continued his news. "There I also decided to quit school and join the air force."

Finally, I could not keep quiet any longer, and I asked, "Why don't you wait until spring and at least get your high school diploma?"

He took off his class ring and handed it to me. "Will you wear this?" Immediately, I put it on my finger, and he answered, "Now I will finish my senior year." Since I knew this ring would be another battle with Mother, I put the ring on a chain and hid it under my sweater.

When Ed knocked on the door with a heart-shaped box of Valentine candy the next week, Mother shouted, "I know you have a class ring around your neck and now a box of candy." She calmed down when my brothers attacked the candy and only left the beautiful box with flowers on top for my keepsake.

Mother and I had battled for years because I wanted a navy blue suit like Terri and her friends wore for Easter Sunday. When I turned sixteen years old, I began working Saturdays at G. C. Murphy. This year, Mother insisted that I contribute my $4 salary from Murphy's for my Easter suit, so I requested a navy blue suit for the third year. When the package arrived, I opened the box from Sears and cried all afternoon because she had ordered small pink and gray houndstooth checks. I felt better when Ed told me how pretty I looked when we met for Easter church service.

The next occasion in Ed's and my relationship would be his graduation from high school. I felt encouraged since Ed had decided to give the local college a try, that is, until I learned that, each time Ed left my house, he lied about going home. He had been cruising and drinking with the guys. Not only were teachers commenting that Ed was not the guy for me but mothers of my friends also counseled me that I was too young to get serious with any boy. Therefore, I broke up with Ed every Friday night and made up every Sunday until the school year ended.

By the time school let out, Mother had left for Piketon, Ohio, where Daddy was still working as an electrician in the uranium plant. She left specific orders for me to take care of Susie, in two weeks take a taxi to the bus terminal, and catch the two o'clock bus for Ohio.

The day before I left for Ohio, I gave Ed his class ring back and told him our values were too different. I had never told him of the pressure

I now got from my friends' parents, my teachers, and the women at church for getting too serious so young. After giving him his class ring, I went on to the back porch to be alone and did not hear Steve and his friend enter. When I looked up and saw Steve's pale face, I snapped, "What is wrong with you?"

He answered, "Ivy, I need to talk to you and Susie."

We all went into the living room, and Steve stood before us, giving an explanation. "I want to be a journalist. I cannot follow in John's footsteps and be an engineer. So I joined the navy and will be leaving for basic training the middle of next week."

I jumped up, screaming, "No, no, no!" and ran to the back porch and began beating the couch. "No, no!"

The one thing I had talked Ed out of doing, my brother did. I could not forget the pain of Uncle Bob dragging his duffel bag during World War II. I felt arms around my shoulders as my brother tenderly said, "Ivy, I need your help! Please do not make this more difficult. Help me to calm Susie, and you have to tell Dad and Mother when you get to Ohio."

The next day, while I waited for time to go to the bus station, I sat on the side porch with Ray's mother, where I could see straight across the intersection to Ed's house. We spent the last hours staring at each other before it was time for me to call a taxi. I cried for Steve and Ed all the way to the bus station. When we got out of the taxi, Susie begged, "Please stop crying! There's a pay telephone. Call Ed."

I dialed his number, and his grandmother told me, "You just missed him. He walked up the street."

After eight hours of crying, when I stepped off the bus, my parents wanted to know why I was crying. I broke the news concerning Steve joining the navy; Mother began crying and had to take to her bed for a few days.

This summer, Daddy parked the small trailer on a knoll under a tree at a ranch. There was a shortage of rooms to rent in the area, so Jan and her husband, who owned the ranch, had created another way to provide rooms by renovating their barn with partitions between beds and bathrooms at each end. To stay out of Mother's way, I volunteered to help Jan; and every morning, we made the workers' beds, cleaned, and sterilized the bathrooms.

This pretty petite woman with long shiny black hair had a happy spirit and was full of life. For the first time, I had an adult who listened to my feelings, and I could tell her how much I missed my ex-boyfriend. She supplied stationery, stamps, and even her address so I could write to Ed without Mother knowing about it.

I wrote and apologized for breaking up with him and told him how much I missed him. His answers to my letters were cool, and I knew that the neighbor from back home who wrote Mother, "Ed and his friends are picking up girls in a nearby town," must be telling the truth.

One of the good things that came out of Steve's joining the navy was it cut our summer trip short since Mother and Daddy planned to visit him during the end of basic training. The morning we prepared to leave, Jan pulled up beside our car, handed me a box, and said, "For helping me clean, here is something to wear in your junior year of high school." I opened a box containing a beautiful blouse and a fancy slip, and suddenly, I remembered the big lie: the day the self-confident petite woman asked what sizes I wore and being ashamed of my body, I gave my sister's size since she was one size smaller than I was. Now as we pulled away, Mother solved the problem by demanding, "Just give those items to Susie. They will fit her."

While we were out of town, John came home from college for the summer. We arrived home to find that John had demolished the house because his fiancée had broken up with him.

The next morning, before Mother could demand that I clean John's room, I decided to start mowing the yard, thinking I might see Ed. Sure enough, in a few minutes, he rode into the yard on his motor scooter and shouted, "Hello! I am glad you are home."

In my youthful ignorance, I did not realize that Mother would be listening to us through the kitchen window. I had the audacity to snap, "Have you had a fun summer?"

His face turned red as he replied, "I invited a girl to the spring formal, if that is what you mean. After all, this is the second summer you have gone off and left me!"

I replied, "Yes, but what about the less-than-desirables you and your friends picked up?" I knew the rumors were true, but I wanted to believe him when he denied them.

On August 30, 1955, for my seventeenth birthday, Ed gave me a birthstone ring and an ankle bracelet. Two days earlier, I had been furious when he grabbed my ankle with both of his hands. I knew Mother would be watching from the kitchen window. Now he apologized, "I had to measure for an ankle bracelet."

When Ed left, Mother's words literally threw me back on the couch: "The birthstone ring better not be an engagement ring." We had never spoken of marriage. We had enough trouble trying to go steady.

While my parents visited Steve, I had the courage to go into the high-class Margaret Spangler ladies' shop and charge an item. They had real crinoline fabric slips, guaranteed to get stiffer with each washing for $7.95 plus tax. I could not believe it when the clerk suggested that I take the slip and make two payments of $4 each. To my surprise, Mother never mentioned the slip or asked about my next two $4 paychecks from G. C. Murphy. To make sure I would be in style at school, I talked Mama into gathering three yards of cotton fabric into skirts to wear over the stiff crinoline.

I began my junior year studying about the largest conference in Geneva, Switzerland, since Roosevelt attended the 1945 Potsdam in Germany. During the month of July, President Eisenhower joined leaders from Great Britain, France, and the Soviet Union without any successful peace from the cold war. Later that fall, the world was shocked by the news that President Eisenhower had suffered a heart attack and was hospitalized.

On November 5, for Ed's nineteenth birthday, his family invited me to dinner. I could not afford nice gifts for him like the ones he had given me. Since entering college, his mom kept a well-stocked wardrobe of the latest fashion for him. He began wearing the famous pink and black, and I added a pink and black stretchy belt for his birthday gift.

The tradition for Ed's birthday consisted of an oyster dinner with the trimmings. The only thing I knew about oysters was when Mother held them up raw before breading and dropped them in oil for her and Daddy and told us children, "You wouldn't like these awful things."

Ed put oysters on my plate and said, "Have you ever tried them?"

I answered, "No."

"Then," he said, "try them before you say you don't like them."

I ate one, and it tasted as good as they smelled cooking, and he told me, "The next time we have shrimp for dinner, I want you to come and try them."

After dinner, Ed and I went to his room to listen to his new hi-fi set. He had begun a great collection of big band sounds of Benny Goodman, Glenn Miller, John Philip Sousa, and Louis Armstrong. I always requested the Mills Brothers' record "Be My Life's Companion" because of a letter Ed had written one dark, cold, snowy night when we broke up for the second time.

It had been just before bedtime when there was a knock on the door. I answered it, and there stood Ed. He handed me a letter and ran. I went to the only private place in the house, the bathroom, and opened it. For the first time, I heard the words to the song: "Be my life's companion, and you will never grow old. I love you so much that you'll never grow old." The next day, we made up without saying another word.

His love for music convinced me to plot, plan, and deceive my parents. I did not know how I became involved with an elite group who lived in the right part of town. However, I knew I would not have any trouble getting permission from Mother to go to a well-known person's home for a pajama party. What I failed to tell her was that the party really consisted of each one going to a nearby town with a date to see the famous star of the song "Blueberry Hill," Fats Domino.

What I had not been prepared for, after all the planning, was the sight when we entered the auditorium. This was my first party where alcohol was served, and I became frightened when I saw the sensual dancing. Unknown to me at the time, the reason I reacted the way I did was that the atmosphere revived the same scary feeling that I had from the years in my parents' bedroom.

Ed sensed I would not enjoy myself, and he tried to keep me busy jitterbugging. Finally, I slipped off to sit in the balcony, and there the view amazed me as I watched the Satch bang on the piano as if there were no keys on it. I could not believe anyone could produce as much perspiration as he did while he sang along with his playing. Eventually, Ed left his fun on the floor and came to sit in the balcony. Once he saw that I had a first-class view of Fats Domino in action, we enjoyed the artist until the crowd shouted, "Let's go home!"

However, the day after Ed's oyster birthday dinner, I felt sluggish and stayed in bed instead of going to church. I knew Ed's dinner had not agreed with my digestive system, especially when I still felt sick and developed diarrhea before daylight on Monday morning. Because Dad had not left yet for Ohio, the sickness embarrassed me until I heard Mother tell him, "When Ivy stayed in bed instead of going to church, I knew she had to be sick. I think we should take her to the hospital."

When we arrived in the overcrowded waiting room, nurses were changing shifts, and the only place left to sit was on a warm radiator. After the lab work, the doctor turned me over to the surgeon for an immediate appendectomy. The orderly helped me onto a gurney and pushed me toward the operating room. I heard Mother tell Daddy, "Well, at least we know she isn't pregnant."

The next thing I knew, Ed's mother was standing over me with a scarf tied around hair rollers. I knew it had to be an emergency for her to be in public with rollers in her hair. As Pam rubbed my face, she told me, "Your sister told Ed that you had been taken to the hospital. He called and demanded that I get to you immediately, or he would skip class."

Being around Nurse Pam in her white uniform had taken away much of the fear I had acquired toward medical people. She also had a way of making me feel comfortable around her. I had enjoyed sitting around their dinner table listening to her tell stories concerning her patients.

Now that she had checked on me, she said, "I have to go home and get ready for my three o'clock shift, and you will be taken good care of."

When she left, Daddy interrupted my peace by teasing, "The hospital bill is $125. You will have to work a lot of Saturdays to pay that off."

Relatives and friends at church and school sent me flowers, gifts, and cards and visited me during the week's stay in the hospital. Even the high school band stopped under my window Friday night as they were marching to the ball field for a football game. With the sound of drumsticks clicking, the band shouted, "Get well, Ivy!" This outpouring of well-wishing revealed that there were people who cared about me.

Life had been moving very fast since Dad, Uncle Bob, John, and Steve left home and spent two summers out of town. However, the greatest change had to be one day after I had recouped from the operation. I came home from school to discover that Mother had done a 180-degree turn from her secluded life by accepting a clerical position at G. C. Murphy's for the holidays.

Her reward for obtaining the position was five new outfits, which she displayed over the couch. Dad had taken her to a nearby town where she purchased five solid-colored gored wool skirts with five matching cardigans and coordinating blouses. I stood speechless, drooling over the stylish outfits, until Mother announced, "Ivy, do not get any ideas. Those are for Susie and me to share."

During this time, Dad had taken some time off from work; he made me uncomfortable by sitting on the back porch and watching television with Ed and me. One evening I walked out into the backyard when Ed was leaving. He backed me up against the brick wall of the porch and said, "I want to tell you something that I never want you to forget." After a long minute, he continued. "I love you." He kissed me and ran.

Not only did I fear that Daddy would hear him but I also had never heard anyone say "I love you" to anyone, and so I thought those three words meant something dirty. I sat down and wrote Ed a letter. "I thought you were a nice boy. I never want to see you again because you talked dirty to me." Ed gently taught me that telling someone you love him or her was a wonderful thing.

Dad returned to his job in Ohio. Mother's departure from home into the marketplace meant that the pinto beans and corn bread could be replaced with plenty of white bread and baloney. Previously, my parents were the only ones who ate sliced bread.

Mother's job created more work for me because I had to keep her work clothes laundered and ironed. Two cold winter nights a week, we filled the wringer washing machine on the cold back porch. However, Tuesdays and Thursdays, I kept warm by ironing Mother's new starched blouses and standing near the furnace and watching lots of television. The family's favorite had to be Walt Disney's specials. He had become a household name with the opening of Disneyland in Anaheim, California.

Ed and I joined the crowds on the first Monday evening in December for the parade that had crowds piling on top of each other from one end of the route to the other. Just before the parade began, the big switch turned the colorful lights on across Main Street for the official opening of the Christmas season.

This, the first December with Mother working outside of the home at Christmas, had to be the most difficult time since I was also working Saturdays at G. C. Murphy, had nightly chores at home, and was studying for midterm exams. In the middle of that busy schedule, I did the unthinkable: I went to my second annual Christmas dance with Ed in the same formal gown that I had worn last year.

At the beginning of the New Year 1956, I began reexamining my relationship with Ed. He had decided not to continue college and reasoned, "All I do is sit in the student union drinking milk and eating honey buns." He began his electrical apprenticeship with his uncle's electrical company while in high school, and now he decided to go work for him full time.

The week of Valentine's Day, another love came into Ed's life, causing the biggest confrontation yet with Mother. His uncle sold him a green 1947 Chevy. After a few weeks, she allowed me to ride with him but only in daylight hours. After a time, Ed convinced her to let me ride home with him after evening church service. Then it wasn't long until she gave me permission to ride home with Ed in his car after the Friday night movies, only if I promised to be in the house fifteen minutes after the movie let out.

Things went well between Ed and me until March, when I agreed to go to a Sunday afternoon movie with a guy in my American history class. Friday night after the movie, I did not have the nerve to tell Ed that I had a date Sunday afternoon. When he pulled up in front of the house, I handed him his ring, jumped out of the car, and ran in the house.

Saturday morning, I could not get my makeup applied without it streaking from the tears running down my cheeks. I missed Ed already! I left the house early, ran to the drugstore, and called him. "I miss you! I am sorry I broke up with you last night! But there is something I have to tell you."

He advised, "Calm down, go to work, and we will talk about it on your lunch hour."

When we met for lunch, I confessed, hoping for mercy, that I had accepted a date with a friend from history class for Sunday afternoon. Ed grabbed my hand, a sad look in his eyes, and he insisted, "Just call and cancel it now."

As a senior in high school, I sat in the drugstore crying because it was foreign for me to say no. For eighteen years, I had never had the right to get angry, give my opinions, or refuse anyone. There were butterflies in my stomach as if I would get in trouble if I called the date off. Of course, at the time, I did not have the vocabulary to explain this to the guy I loved. He gave in to me to keep peace. "Go ahead on the date."

I had the nerve to ask, "Will you still go to church with me afterward?"

On Sunday afternoon, Mike parked his father's shiny brand-new black car in front of our house. After he met my parents, I got in the car and sat as close to the passenger's door as possible. At the intersection, I saw Ed standing in front of his house watching us. I knew my date wondered what happened to that fun-loving girl from American history class. I would not let him hold my hand in the movie or take me for something to eat afterward. I realized it would have been much kinder to call off the date.

As promised, my faithful boyfriend came to take me to church. John, home from college for the weekend, walked through the living room, looked at Ed, and said, "You are crazy for letting her treat you like that."

However, the very next Friday night, I gave Ed his school ring back *again*. This time, it was because one of my teachers gave me some advice: "You really should be dating an educated person."

The very next Saturday morning, a college sophomore named Barry, who worked part-time next door to G. C. Murphy, asked me to have lunch with him. He had everything a person could want in a companion. He was a handsome tall blond-haired young man, and more important to society, he was studying to be a coach. My high school coach had no respect for any guy who did not play sports. After lunch with "Mr. Perfect," he invited me to a movie on Friday night, and I accepted.

On Friday night, when I opened the front door, there sat a new 1956 Plymouth that belonged to Barry's father. Even though Mother worked next door to him, her face went pale when she saw him instead of Ed.

After a brief exchange of words with my parents, he drove straight to a drive-in movie outside of town. While one hand turned off the engine, his other arm pulled me toward him. I had not had time to look around or even talk when I found myself deep in kisses.

After the movie, Barry stopped at the popular drive-in for Cokes, and Ed pulled alongside us in his 1947 Chevy. He gunned his engine and took off, spinning wheels and throwing gravels on the new Plymouth.

Barry was not only athletic but was also good in singing. Some nights, with his arms around me, he sang "Dungaree Doll"; "You, You, You"; "Earth Angel"; and "The Great Pretender." When he opened the car door and helped me in, I felt as if I were entering a dream world. I did not understand sexual desires and what this kind of setting could lead to, and I could not refuse all the kissing. In my ignorance, every night, I requested my date to sing my favorite songs "He" and "It Is No Secret What God Can Do."

Finally, Barry began noticing me for more than just having lips. On our lunch hour from our jobs the Saturday before Easter, he volunteered to walk across the street to the small boutique and help me find a red hat.

This year, Mother ordered a light blue three-piece suit from Sears for me. The box jacket and long straight skirt had a coordinating blouse that matched the lining of the jacket. The white background fabric had multicolor spring flowers, and I had chosen the red color to accessorize. Barry picked the red hat that he thought looked best on me before he surprised me by saying, "I am going to sunrise service with you in the morning."

Every date had been the same until one Friday night when he took me to an indoor movie on Main Street. We got out of the movie earlier than from the outdoor movie, and he suggested a ride, so I agreed. He drove ten miles to the college that he attended, but instead of driving around campus, he turned up a little narrow country road. Suddenly,

I remembered hearing students whispering about what happened at the old dam. For the first time, I took charge of the situation. "Is this the road that leads to the old dam?"

"Yes."

I became furious and demanded, "Turn this car around now and take me home."

He said, "I have to go until I find a place to turn around."

I shouted, "No! I want to turn around now."

On that narrow, one-lane path, he drove back and forth until he got the car turned around and headed toward home. He began apologizing. "I'm sorry that I have upset you." Then I realized that I missed the security I felt when I was with Ed.

The next Sunday night, I walked down Main Street with my friend Maggie, and Ed pulled up to the curb and said, "Hey, you girls want a ride?"

Maggie jumped in the car, and I could not believe how familiar they were with each other. I sat as close to the door as I could. I wondered why Ed drove straight to Maggie's house. I had to get out of the car to let her out, and she hit me on the arm as she passed.

I leaned back in the '47 Chevy, and it felt warm and safe. When Ed pulled up in front of my house, very formally, he said, "It was good to be with you again."

The next week, in spite of rumors of Maggie dating my ex-boyfriend, we went to the high school graduation and had a sleepover at her house. Maggie and I dressed in our Easter outfits, except for the hats, and walked to the high school. I wanted to see my friend and neighbor Sally graduate.

In her senior year of high school, Sally had broken up with Ray and married a white-collar man. Sally had given in to the same pressures from teachers as I had and traded her first love for one who measured up to the proper standards of the community. Nevertheless, Sally told me when she became engaged to her new boyfriend, "At least he doesn't have grease under his fingernails from working on hot rods."

Going to see our friends graduate, Maggie and I were more anxious than ever for the next year when we would march across the stage and get our diploma. As fate would have it, Maggie and I walked out of the high school just as Ray pulled up in his fancy custom Chevy and asked,

"Would you two girls like to go for a hamburger and Coke?" Maggie pushed me into the car first.

There was nothing cheap about Ray. He drove to a nearby town to a drive-in restaurant where most of the parking places were filled with graduates ordering over the speakers. As we waited for our turn, we listened to Ray explain in detail about the custom job he had done on his hot rod.

While we ate, all three of us laughed and reminisced about the spring we went to the circus together. Then Ray began telling Maggie about the night he took me for a ride in his hot rod and I talked him into letting me drive. Since I had never been behind a wheel on a narrow, two-lane street, I drove into a woman's lawn. Ray laughed as he reported, "It was a week later the woman who lived in that house died. I know Ivy gave her a heart attack when she saw the headlights heading toward her living room."

As we started for home, I asked, "Ray, let me drive."

He replied, "Not in this traffic. Wait until we get out of town."

He pulled over to the side of a long straight stretch of road, and we traded seats. I began driving as I had seen the people in the movies do—just push the gas pedal and turn the steering wheel back and forth. As I started up a grade, a car came barreling over the hill, and the oncoming lights blinded me.

The next thing I knew, I had gone across the highway and started down a mountain where a tree stopped the car. One of my red shoes went off my foot and out the door, which had flown open. I had enough sense to run around the car and be in the passenger's side before a car stopped to help.

A carload of college guys celebrating graduation stopped, looked over the situation, took chains from their car's trunk, and pulled Ray's car back to flat land. The banged-up customized car sounded like a tin lizzie until Ray beat the fenders away from the wheels. Maggie cried, I shook, and Ray put his arm around me as he drove toward town. The way he was holding me made me think, *I am obligated to him, and I know that I will have to marry him now.*

As we approached town and entered the circle around the courthouse, Ed entered from another direction. He motioned for us to pull over to the curb. When he walked over to our crumbled-up car, his face went red when he saw Ray's arm around me. He demanded, "You girls get in my car now."

When I stepped out, Ed pointed at Ray's car and asked, "Ivy, did you do that?"

I stood on the sidewalk with only one shoe on and cried, "Yes! And I am obligated to Ray for the rest of my life."

He repeated, "Get in my car now."

I felt relief from the pressure of owing Ray when I heard Ed tell him, "I am sorry she wrecked your fancy car, but don't you worry. The first thing in the morning, we will begin restoring it."

Ed drove us to Maggie's house and demanded, "Go in the house and stay there."

We ran up the stairs, and her parents called from the living room, "What's the hurry?"

My friend shouted, "As soon as we get into our pajamas, we'll be down for milk." I envied her when we went back downstairs and she sat in her father's lap for comfort.

After breakfast the next morning, I walked home in my tennis shoes and jeans and worried that Mother would find out that I had lost one of my dress shoes. As I neared the neighborhood, I heard the beating of metal. True to his word, Ed had begun to help Ray beat the dents out of the fenders of his hot rod. I stopped, and Ed shared with me, "We went out to where you went off the road looking for the fender skirts. It is nothing but a miracle that the tree caught part of the car, or you three would have gone down that mountain and died."

Ed did not attempt to restore our relationship because Dad would be home at the end of the week, and we were going to spend the summer in *Baltimore*! Ed complained, "This is the third summer you've left town. I have never spent a summer with you."

However, I did accept an invitation before leaving town to attend the wedding of a mutual friend with Barry and his sister Amber. Instead of going to the reception, he took us to a drive-in for food, and it surprised me when he asked, "Do you have to leave for the summer?"

I assured him that I had to do whatever my parents told me. He asked, "Will you send your address to Amber? We will write you."

Daddy's sister and my biological mother, Martha, had moved back to town from the West Coast just weeks before school ended and was staying at our house. Now that she and her second husband were divorcing, she needed a place to stay with her two preschool children, and she was going to house-sit while we were out of town. This would give her time to find a place to live. One day as I stood with Martha and her two children, Mother commented, "How nice to see you all together finally."

My worst nightmare ever was riding toward the "forbidden city," Baltimore, with Daddy driving the car and Mother sitting beside him. The thought went through my mind: *In the eleven years since leaving Baltimore, I had only told one person about the rape.*

Just last fall, I came home from the town's Halloween street party and found Susie in the downstairs bedroom, crying. John and Susie both had the reputation of *not* crying. Therefore, seeing my sister in tears frightened me. That October week, Steve had brought a friend home with him from the navy. Susie, Steve, his friend, and I had separated during the street dancing. I tried to comfort my sister and demanded, "Tell me why you are crying!"

She sobbed. "When I got home, Mother accused me of being in a motel with Steve's friend."

Stunned, angry, and in a rage, I began spewing out feelings of stored anger. "Susie, listen to me, you have heard her accuse me of lying in school playgrounds with boys and being in motels at six years of age."

Susie lifted her head and sobbed, "Yes."

Without thinking, I allowed the unthinkable to spew from my mouth to comfort my sister. "When we lived in Baltimore, Mother watched Daddy rape me and told him to take me to the hospital, and then they accused an innocent man of doing it."

Susie stopped crying and sat up on the edge of the bed, and for the first time, we clung to each other for support. In my youthful ignorance, I, of all people, should have learned that nothing happened in that house without Mother's knowledge. For the first time, she never came in the room to take Susie.

After a long, eight-hour hot (before car air-conditioning) trip to Baltimore, two strange occurrences happened to set my nerves on edge. First, Dad stopped the car at a playground and told Susie and me to get out and play. In the upcoming fall, Susie would be a junior, and

I would be a senior in high school, and our parents sat in the car and watched us. As I sat on a swing, the familiarity of the place became overwhelming, especially when I looked at the black wrought iron fence; and in my mind, I could see a man staring at me through the bars.

Second, when Daddy pulled up in front of a block of town houses, I nearly fainted from shock when Mother instructed, "Susie, you sit in the car. And, Ivy, follow us upstairs." I followed them up the stairs of 2220 East North Street, and the only thing I feared was being alone with these two people. After walking through the furnished three rooms, the questions began to fly. From the weird looks on their faces, I began trembling when Mother demanded to know if anything looked familiar.

When I shook my head no, Daddy fired, "Do you think you have ever been here before?"

I just said, "It's too hot up here."

Mother commanded, "Go downstairs and get Susie." I ran down the steps two at a time.

We found ourselves crowded, hot, and without a television in an upstairs three-room apartment. The first time Mother hung the washed clothes out the kitchen window, I stood spellbound as I remembered a woman pinning items to the pulley line, and I even remembered the family that came to visit and how I tried to trick the neighbors by ringing their doorbells.

That morning, Mother gave me directions to go to the corner grocery store. "Go out the front door, turn left, cross the intersection, and get a pack of cigarettes at the little corner grocery."

As I began walking back to the apartment from the store, the memory of this store made me wonder if at the other end of the block was a candy store. I passed the apartment and walked to the other end of the block and across the intersection, and there sat an empty building that had housed the candy store where the mother accused me of slapping her daughter.

The pressure that I lived under for the last fifteen years might have been one of the main reasons I did not connect the dots of my real mother returning to our hometown with spending the summer in an upstairs apartment in Baltimore, the stores, the beach, and the doctor's office. I would have never dreamed that this summer was all about me admitting if I remembered my real mother. The summer mysteries added another strange piece to the puzzle. Dad began working in Delaware and visited us in Baltimore on weekends.

After he left the first week, Mother told me, "Dad thinks you are too nervous, and he wants me to take you to the doctor."

Mother left Susie with a neighborhood girl to terrorize the city, and we left for the doctor's office. This was another excuse to see if I remembered the office. Strangely, Mother sat in the waiting room for a few minutes before announcing to me, "I will tell Daddy that the doctor just wants you to read and relax. Do you remember this office?"

Nervously, I replied, "No!"

Once outside, the situation became even stranger when Mother instructed, "Go find a job so you can purchase your school clothes."

She and I boarded a bus for downtown, and Mother demanded, "You take the left side of the street, I will take the right side, and we will see which one of us finds a job first."

The personnel in W. T. Grant asked if I would be interested in working behind the luncheonette counter for the summer. I agreed that I would.

I waited at the designated area until Mother appeared, smiling. She had accepted a position at the notions counter of a department store across the street. When we returned home, Susie and her friend Fran had roamed and explored all day, and Susie asked if she could get a job also. Mother assured Susie, "You don't need to get a job. I will take you on a shopping spree for your school clothes before we go back home."

Every morning, Mother made sure we left early enough to stop in the corner drugstore for breakfast before the stores opened. Here was where I forgot all my troubles. I climbed up on the high stool at the counter, watched, and listened to the other workers hustling and bustling in and out of the drugstore for their breakfast. I felt important, excited, secure, and safe, like one of the crowd.

The tips I got from the luncheon counter I shared with my sister and her new friend, Fran, by hiring them to purchase items for me from the grocery store and mail my letters back home. I had answered only one of Barry's letters because, immediately, I began missing Ed and grieving over our separation. To ease the pain, I began firing off letters to him once we settled down to a schedule in Baltimore. At first, Ed answered my letters, and then the letters stopped. I buried the pain in my heart with work, movies, or an Orioles' baseball game at Memorial Stadium with Betty, who lived next door.

Betty lived at home with her parents, and most evenings after work, she and her mother sat on the front porch trying to keep cool. After the sermon I preached to Ed about drinking beer, I was surprised that I did not react to Betty's parents. Just about every night, her mother walked across the street two or three times a night to the corner tavern and carried back about a third of a gallon of draft beer in a pickle jar.

Two doors from Betty lived a family who introduced me to their grandson, Rod, visiting on a weekend leave from the navy. Rod and I were sitting on the front porch swing, getting acquainted, when he invited me to a movie on Saturday night. The first thing that ran through my mind when I accepted his invitation was "What will Daddy and Mother say?"

However, they appeared at that moment, and Mother embarrassed me by shouting over four porches, "Ivy, go upstairs this minute and stay with Susie." I jumped up like a two-year-old and ran home.

I was not sure if the sailor would show up on Saturday night or not. If he did, I was not going to tell Mother about the date and pretend that he stopped by on his own. I sat on the porch until dark, and he never showed up.

This was just one rejection too many, and I broke down. I cried aloud as I grieved from very deep down in my soul. Occasionally, Mother would scream, "Why are you crying!"

For the first time in my life, I did not answer her. I could never have put those uncontrollable feelings into words at that time in my life. To add insult to injury, the next weekend, the sailor's mother made a point of stopping to explain, "Because your mother called you so rudely, my son decided not to come to your house."

During that turbulent summer of 1956, I saved $80 and purchased my school clothes from department stores instead of ordering from the Sears, Roebuck & Co. catalog. My favorite purchase had to be the medium green wool skirt with a cardigan to match. However, my satisfaction was diminished as I watched Mother purchase Susie many new pretty outfits.

During my last day and my last hour working at W. T. Grant, I heard a voice from behind me say, "Hey, I need help over here."

I turned, and to my delight, there sat Steve smiling at me. Unknown to me, he had made plans to visit us before being stationed in Illinois. Instantly, I became popular as single women gathered around the counter, waiting for me to introduce them to the handsome sailorman.

The night before leaving for home, Steve took Susie and me to the movie *Oklahoma!* starring Shirley Jones and Gordon MacRae. Steve achieved his objective at the beginning of the movie. We felt as if we were on top of the airplane as it flew low over the rows of cornfields, and we put our hands up to keep the stalks from hitting us in the face. Afterward, he topped the evening off by treating us to 10¢ hamburgers at a nearby café.

The next afternoon, Steve informed me that he and I were going to ride home on the Greyhound bus out of Baltimore since our new school clothing took up so much room in the car that there was not enough room for us.

That evening on the bus, as Steve laid his head against the window, sleeping, the guy across the aisle began a casual conversation with me. Suddenly, Steve sat up, gave the guy a dirty look, and said, "Ivy, trade seats with me." We traveled and sat in the bus terminal for a total of twelve hours before we arrived in our hometown and got off the bus on Main Street.

After being in a big busy city, our hometown seemed dead at three in the morning until Steve surprised me. He stopped, and pointing up to the sky, he asked, "Have you ever seen the Big and Little Dipper?"

I replied, "What? A dipper?"

He spent the next few minutes opening my mind to the sky by outlining the stars for me. When we arrived at the corner, I could see Ed's car in his driveway. Once under the streetlight, I felt relieved seeing that Ray's car was completely restored and had new fender skirts. By the time Steve and I got home, Dad and the family had been home and asleep for hours.

Martha found an apartment that would be available on the first of September. She had accomplished mission impossible by installing a telephone in our home. Uncle Bob's wife, Pat, worked at Murphy's, and she had told Barry that I was back home and gave him my telephone number. Immediately, my secret mother, Martha, encouraged Barry to keep calling me even though I had made it known to everyone "Do not call me to the telephone if Barry calls."

The first day at home from Baltimore, I sneaked into the hall and dialed Ed's phone to learn later that he had told his family, "I do not want to talk to Ivy."

Whenever I saw his car at the four-way stop, I would run like blazes into the middle of the street; and to avoid me, he would turn left instead of coming straight out the street to my house. I happened to be at the front door one day as he passed, and I ran out screaming, "Ed, stop!"

He did. I walked toward the car, and he smiled and said, "I saw your daddy's car, and I figured you were back in town. I am running late. I really need to go."

He could not look me in the eye. The final blow to my emotions was when he spoke with coolness and formality, and I managed to save face by saying, "I'll let you go. Maybe we can talk later."

I ran into the house and up the steps, and I leaned over to finish making Steve's bed when a flood burst inside of me. I never thought to check to see if I had enough privacy to let go of my emotions. It never dawned on me that I lay next to an open window and that the whole neighborhood could hear as I collapsed on the bed and wailed from deep within my soul with the sounds of a caged animal wanting to be freed. I did not know how long I lay there releasing the built-up anguish from my soul when I felt arms around me. Then I heard Ed say, "Now, now, everything will be all right."

I snapped out of the deep, dark pit as fast as lightning from the shock of a boy being upstairs in a bedroom with me. I sobbed, "How did you get up here?"

His arms were around me, holding me close, as he explained, "I drove around the block, and when I came back by your house, I could hear you screaming from the street. Don't be afraid. Your mother told me to come up here. She and Susie were sitting in the living room listening to you."

I couldn't believe that I did not get into serious trouble for that outburst. Without asking permission, I agreed to go to the movies with Ed that evening. After he picked me up, he threw a stack of his letters toward me. He had written to me, and all the letters had been returned to him. I looked at the address on the letters and said, "This isn't the address I sent you."

Immediately, I became angry with my sister and her friend. I trusted and even paid them to mail these letters. What they did was to add extra numbers to the return address on the letters I had written Ed.

To calm our minds, after the movie, Ed suggested, "Let's go to the old mill dam tomorrow after church and relax." To stay out of trouble with Dad and Mother, I asked my friend Maggie and her future husband, Ted, to go with us.

I always had a great time when Ed's family invited me to the old mill for picnics, and they made sure there were plenty of inner tubes to float around the river. If they didn't cook out, we ate in the small snack bar, which also had a jukebox.

Before beginning the thirty-minute drive down the winding roads, Ed stopped at the service station where an attendant filled our tank, checked the oil, and cleaned the windshield. Ed took the tire gauge and checked the air in the tires before going into the station to pay for the gas. While we waited, the three of us complained about rumors that the price of gasoline would be going from 26¢ a gallon to 30¢.

Ed acted very strangely as he got back in the car and said, "Help me find my car keys."

He went back in the station, and the three of us searched the car. I opened the glove compartment, and there lay a letter to Ed from Mattie. I dared the couple in the backseat to tell Ed that I had put the letter in my blouse. When Ed got back in the car, he said, "The keys were in my pocket."

Before arriving at the mill, Ed asked, "Ivy, why are you so quiet?"

Lying, I said, "Oh, just thinking about the news that the gasoline price is going higher."

At the old mill, I jumped out of the car and shouted, "I am going to change into my bathing suit."

I ran into one of the small white dressing buildings and began to read the letter Ed had received from a woman I had never heard of. "I miss you and the wonderful summer we had together. When will you come to see me soon? If you will marry me, I promise to work and support you."

Maggie came into the building, shook me, and made me get into in my swimsuit. Then she picked up the letter to read what had me in shock. I finally got into my bathing suit, walked to the car, and put the letter back. I controlled myself enough to get in an inner tube, set out to sail, and help fill the river with my tears.

About half an hour after Ed disappeared down the river, I came out of the water and went to the snack bar. There sat Ed in one of the old wooden booths, listening to a song on the jukebox, "Breaking Up Is Hard to Do." The tears began to flow again as I walked to the other side of the small room and sat in another booth. Finally, Ed came over, sat beside me, and said, "I know you read the letter."

I swallowed my pride and asked, "Can you tell me who this Mattie is?"

He played with the straw in the short Coke bottle as he related. "I met her at a party this summer while she attended beautician school. Just before you came home, she completed the training and chose a shop out of the area."

I swallowed even harder as I asked the loaded question, "Are you going to marry her?"

He looked at me and dropped his head before answering, "My grandmother was upset this summer because I stayed out until the wee hours. Marriage is her idea, not mine." He took my hand. "You know who I want to marry."

The four of us were exhausted by the time we arrived back in town. I dressed, went to training union, and met Ed for church service. I sat beside him in church, feeling relaxed and calm that our troubles were behind us until he drove me home. When he walked me to the door, he asked, "Will you go steady with me?"

I had been suspicious of the fact that he had not been wearing his class ring. I softly asked, "If I can wear your class ring again."

He looked down, kicked his foot, and said, "The other day, while I was working with my uncle, I lost that ring."

Here we go again. For some reason, that excuse infuriated me, and I stated before shutting the door, "Well, I don't want to date you until you put your class ring back on my finger."

The next day, when I had not heard from Ed, I knew he had gone to get his class ring from Mattie. Late in the afternoon, I talked Susie into walking out to Ed's house to see if he was home. His grandmother told her, "Ed has gone to get an engine for his model airplane from his cousin." Common sense told me that, if that had been the case, he would have insisted that I go with him because he had talked about taking me to Beckley to meet his legitimate father.

I watched television until after dark and started up the steps when I heard a knock on the door. I opened it, and there stood a very distraught young man. He put his class ring on my finger as he lied, "Look what I found today."

"Oh, I hoped you loved me enough to drive four hours round-trip to get it from your friend."

He looked relieved and replied, "I did! It was awful! When I finally found the beauty shop where Mattie worked, she took off early and invited me to her apartment. As she began fixing us a dinner, I broke the news of why I had come to see her. She handed me the ring, and I turned and left her crying."

I apologized. "I'm sorry that I put you through that, but this ring means a lot to us, and I didn't want to lose it."

By my eighteenth birthday that August 30, 1956, the events of the summer had made me feel much older. For my birthday, Ed gave me something that I had always wanted: a gold cross on a chain. The next week, he began working as a Carman helper on the Virginia Railroad, and I began my senior year in high school.

By the end of the month, the college preparatory schedule had me in another kind of tailspin. Ed sat at my dining room table trying his best to teach me physics while Mother and Susie watched television on the back porch. Unexpectedly, Ed interrupted, "I am tired of breaking up with you. Do you realize that we have never spent a summer together? Please say you will run away with me and marry me so we'll never have to spend another summer apart."

Emotionally drained, I said, "Yes!"

When he asked, "Will you set the date?" I looked across the round antique oak table to where a yardstick with the logo of my grandfather's lumber supply shop printed on it lay on one of his calendars. I reached for it and studied the months before committing myself. "What about over the Christmas holidays? Look here, beginning the third week of December, I get out of school half days to work at Murphy's."

Ed smiled and agreed, "That gives me four months to get settled in my job, but give me a date."

I said, "How about December 21?" We shook hands; it was a deal.

Since Mother worked at Murphy's with many of my high school friends, it became very important that the elopement be kept a secret. Believe me, during the next three months, the excitement grew as I told Jill, and she screamed, "Wonderful! I will plan the bridal shower." Suddenly, that made it real that I planned to elope! She continued. "Okay, we have to start working on the list of high school girls you want to attend the shower during the Christmas holidays." I agreed without realizing that meant she would mail fifty invitations at least a week before I eloped.

The realization that I had promised to run away with Ed frightened me, and I went to visit my friend Sally, who had gotten married. She got excited, encouraged me, and even laid out an escape plan. "You leave for school, go in Ray's back door, and watch out the window until your family leaves for the day. Once everyone has left, I will meet you and help you pack before Ed arrives. While you are gone, I am going to organize a neighborhood bridal shower for January."

Planning to elope during the middle of the 1956–57 senior school years, I lost interest in the fact we were the first senior class in a modern brand-new school building. The new building held no fond memories, and my mind focused on marriage. The new high school also was so far that I could not go home for lunch or do all the morning chores.

We no longer studied history but became part of it. For the first time in history, five African Americans enrolled in the junior class, and there were sixteen sophomores. To the best of my memory, there were no untoward incidents.

I had a calm and peaceful first semester in my senior year. I was voted president of the Girls' Athletic Association (GAA), and for the third straight year, our team won the basketball tournament. However, this year, Susie and her rough junior class team gave us a battle, hitting, scratching, pulling hair, and trying to take the championship from us.

Ed met me after school, and we usually walked to the drugstore. One night in early December, he held my hand and led me across Main Street. I was soaking up the hometown Christmas atmosphere with the man I loved. We had not had a cross word since setting the elopement date.

Since there was not a parking place in town with all the Christmas shoppers, Ed took me to a dark alley where he parked in the gas company's lot. In the darkness of night, he told me, "Open the glove compartment."

I grabbed for the latch and opened it, and there by the little inside light sat a ring box. I took the beautiful velvet ring box in my hand and ruined the moment by quizzing him, "Is the wedding band in here?"

When he nodded *yes*, I became irritated. "You know it's bad luck for a bride to see her wedding ring before getting married!"

He reached over, took the box, and removed the wedding band. It never dawned on me that my future husband might not know that those kinds of things were important to a girl. I opened the box to view the beautiful engagement ring, and it looked gigantic compared to most of the girls' diamonds in high school.

When my fiancé put the ring on my finger, we engaged in the best and longest kiss that I ever had. Then he asked, "Do you mind having a sandwich at my house?"

As we drove toward his home, he explained that his parents had helped him shop for the rings. "You didn't reveal our elopement plans, did you?" As we walked up on his front porch, he assured me they didn't know, and I felt like a queen when we entered the house.

The family, eagerly waiting for us, took turns hugging and welcoming me to the family. The excitement was too much for me, and I couldn't enjoy the grilled cheese sandwich. When time came for me to go back to work, my happy future in-laws all hugged me good-bye.

When Ed and I got back in the car, I happened to think, *Mother!* Ed informed me that he had to go to the railroad union meeting that night and wouldn't be able to pick Mother and me up after work.

We returned to town, and I saw Steve standing in front of the drugstore, and I told Ed, "Look, even Steve is home from the navy for this big announcement."

I jumped out of the car and called, "Hey, Steve, I need to speak to you."

He followed me into a storefront, and he questioned, "Ivy, what is the matter?"

I stepped to the other side of the window. He followed and I said, "I need you to do me a big favor!"

He put his arm around my shoulders and said, "Oh, what has happened?"

Then I held out my left hand and cried, "I am so afraid of Mother! Please talk her into letting me keep the ring. You know if you approve, she will too."

Steve took my hand and, ever so tenderly, moaned, "Oh, Dot. Oh, Dot." When I felt his disapproval, I pulled my hand from his and began rubbing the ring against the store window. He broke the tension. "Haven't you heard? Diamond will cut glass, and one that large will definitely cut this window."

He put his arm around me and continued. "What would you have done if I hadn't gotten a weekend pass?" He took my hand and said, "Come on, let's go and announce your engagement."

He went into Murphy's ahead of me, and I shouted, "I have to go clock in."

When I arrived at Mother's counter, I knew by the way she curled her lips that Steve had given her the news. I held my hand where she could see the ring, and her only comment was "Don't you think you better get back to work before the manager fires you?"

After we returned home from work that night, for the first time *ever*, she announced, "Ivy will sleep with me tonight."

When I got in her bed, I turned to Jell-O as I lay so close to the far edge of the bed that I almost fell off during the night. She began immediately, "If you wait until June to get married, I will give you a church wedding."

I had a one-track mind when it came to Mother. As I lay there, all I could think of was that she needed someone to do the house chores and that she would never let me get married. Then on the other hand, she might give me some sort of wedding if Granddad Ooking poured money into her pocket. Somehow, I survived the night without agreeing with her.

The next morning, I walked into church, and people flocked around to see my ring. After Sunday school, I put on my choir robe and stood in line, waiting to enter the choir loft. One of the college girls came and stood with me. She had been engaged in high school, broke it off, and dated my brother. She asked, "Have you and Ed set a date?"

I answered, "Yes, December 21. However, last night, my mother asked me to wait and have a June wedding."

As serious as any person had ever spoken to me, she replied, "Take my advice. Once you postpone, you will do it again and again until you lose the person you love."

As we took our places in the choir loft, I thought of the lonely summers when I had missed Ed. I looked through the congregation to find him sitting in our usual place. When he finally had the nerve to look at me after running out on me the night before, I gave him a big smile.

After the service, I ran out front to meet him, and the first thing he wanted to know was "What did your mother have to say?"

"Steve told her for me, and she asked me to wait until June for a church wedding."

"You aren't going to let her trick you, are you?"

"No!"

I had taken one paycheck to purchase a $3.95 waltz-length light yellow nightgown. One Saturday night, when I worked with my uncle Bob's wife, she informed me, "Your mother found your trunk packed with your new gown."

When Aunt Martha moved, she had left her old college trunk in my closet, and I put the gown in the trunk on top of my summer clothes. At the last minute, Sally and I were going to pack the new winter items that I had purchased in Baltimore. I knew that Mother knew every plan I had because she worked with many of my school friends. She must have told Steve because he gave me a serious threat: "If you elope, take everything with you because you will not get back in the house."

Ed had not waited until Christmas to give me the diamond, invitations to a bridal shower were already in the mail, and I had reported I would be off from work to my employer. When I told the personnel manager that I would not be in for the next four days, she warned, "If you plan to be away during Christmas, you will never work here again."

To add to the rising tension, the night before I eloped, Mother moved back upstairs to her and Daddy's old bedroom. For the first time ever, she began chatting with me from her room. "This summer, we might need to do some painting."

I made stupid comments. "We will have to wait and talk about it after tomorrow."

As Mother continued talking, my thoughts went back over the many nights I had slept in this room with my sister. Some nights we laughed, cried, and talked until Mother shouted, "Girls, I don't want to hear another noise from in there." Sometimes we were having too much fun playing house. If our heads were covered, that meant we were in the house; uncovered meant we were sitting on the porch. When we both were on the porch, we talked, and sometimes we would laugh so hard that we could not get our breath. Usually, out of the dark, a belt would fly across my body, and Susie would begin screaming because she knew she might get a lick next. It would be days before she would speak to me again.

The next morning, Friday, my wedding day, I pretended to be going to school a half day and work at Murphy's the other half. But I turned the corner and ran in the back door of Ray's house, where his mother and I watched from her front window as Susie and Mother left the house. I ran out the front door and started across the street, and Sally ran after me. We ran up the steps and down the hall, and we finished filling the trunk. By the time Ed arrived, we had everything ready.

Sally bade us farewell, and Ed turned the car around and drove toward his house. I could not believe his mother standing on the porch waving. I looked at him. "You weren't supposed to tell them."

He commented, "Someone had to pack my suitcase, and besides, half the town knows."

Ed looked handsome in his dark suit and white shirt. I felt guilty wearing the blue suit with the hat that Barry had chosen. We drove straight to a hospital in a nearby town and had our blood tests, and the lab tech said, "Your tests will be ready in the morning."

I went weak in the knees! Outside I pleaded, "There is no way you can take me back to my parents. If we do not get married, you have to promise that you will always pretend that we are."

He took me walking through the streets of the little town, and what a romantic scene it was. Hand in hand, we walked up and down steep sidewalks toward the shopping area in the cool, crisp weather. He suggested walking into JCPenney. Just inside the door was a clerk marking down pretty winter robes, and Ed told me to pick one as a wedding gift.

We hurried back to the car, drove to the outskirts of town, and had a sandwich at the drive-in. As we waited in silence, I thought of the night we had eaten here after Steve and Ed's graduation from high school. The last time I had been here, I wrecked Ray's car.

When the carhop hooked the tray onto the side of the door, my husband-to-be handed me a hot dog, but I couldn't eat. I asked him to lean forward so I could put my food back on the tray, and I dropped ketchup on the back of his white shirt. He hadn't brought an extra one. I tried to clean it off, and finally the tension was broken, and we had a good laugh.

Ed decided to look for a motel, and he warned me, "Whether you like it or not, you will have to put on the wedding band before we are married." I asked him to put the ring on my finger and give me a kiss before registering at the motel as husband and wife.

Once in the motel room, I felt awkward until Ed took me in his arms and kissed me. All the feelings I had for him overcame the fears of the day. He began taking my blouse off. I had learned about menstrual cycles in health class as a way of birth control and that I could get pregnant this time of the month. Therefore, I ruined the moment by saying, "Do you have protection to prevent me from getting pregnant?"

Ed snapped at that moment and left the room. I sat waiting for him to return, but an hour passed before he opened the door and shouted, "Come on, I found a bar restaurant that has great hot dogs."

The fact he had gone to a bar instead of purchasing protection made me feel as if I had been slapped in the face. I put my blouse back on, dropped my head in defeat, and walked out of the motel. It would take years before I would be free to express my feelings. Ten minutes later, I sat on a barstool nibbling on a hot dog and watching the nightly news on the television hanging over the bar.

Thinking back on the return to the motel, Ed, usually quiet, must have had drinks at the bar before he came to get me because he pointed to a pay telephone and shouted, "Okay, time to call our parents."

I knew both Daddy and John would be home this Friday night for the Christmas holidays. At the telephone, I bargained with my husband-to-be, "You call my family, and I will call yours."

I hated to lie to Ed's grandmother when she answered the telephone. "Hi, Mama, we are married."

She pricked my conscience when she asked, "You got your blood test? I sure wish you kids had waited until tomorrow because that's the day I married Ed's grandfather."

Next, Ed made the dreaded call to my family, and I heard him in the telephone booth say, "Ivy and I eloped today, everything is fine, and we will see you Sunday."

Ed and I told lies to our parents, and we went back to the room to get ready for bed. My husband undressed for the shower, and for the first time, I saw a nude man. The biblical passage 1 Corinthians 14:20 described how I survived child abuse, and it still very much shocked me the first time I saw my husband nude: "Brothers, stop thinking like children. In regard to evil, be infants, but in your thinking be adults." Concerning evil, I had grown up in my parents' bedroom and came out as innocent as an infant.

Another surprise was that Ed did not act interested in romance. He looked sad. I felt sympathy for him and tried to hold him close. I behaved defensively when Ed commented, "Boy, if the guys at the railroad could see me now, would they ever have a laugh."

I didn't understand because I didn't know that a man could be impotent. He explained that the idea that I could get pregnant caused it. I replied, "I don't think you should go to work and share intimate things and have the men laughing at us."

He apologized. "I am only teasing." He warmed my heart when he looked at his wedding band and told me, "Now I have a gold ring to shine on my black hands like the other guys at the railroad." We fell asleep holding each other.

Early the next morning, we raced to get the results of our blood work and drove for the license before the courthouse closed at noon. As we walked up the sidewalk toward the courthouse, several elderly men sitting on a bench smiled and said, "First door on your left." We went through the door to our left, and we were the only couple applying.

When Ed told the woman that we would like to get a marriage license, she replied, "How old are you?"

We both lied, "Twenty-one."

I thought my troubles were over until I almost told the truth when the woman asked, "What is your occupation?"

The first words that wanted to come out of my mouth were "I go to high school." Quickly, my mind told me you would not be in school at twenty-one years old, and I recovered with "I work at Murphy's."

I still was not out of the woods because she almost stumped me again when she smiled and asked, "How did you manage to get off work this time of the year?"

This time, I did tell the truth when I told her, "I had to choose between my job and him."

We rushed out of the courthouse to find the address of Reverend Bradshaw, whom the woman at the courthouse recommended. It was noon when we knocked on his door, and when he opened the door, a wonderful aroma of food flowed out. Ed asked, "Will you marry us?"

Pastor Bradshaw replied, "If you can wait until I finish my anniversary luncheon. Today is my twenty-fifth wedding anniversary."

Index

A

abuse, ix, 17, 65, 69, 87, 89, 101, 128, 177
  child, 177
Alfred (uncle of Ivy), 13–14, 48, 52, 62
Appalachian Mountains, 3, 5
Ashley (friend of Ivy), 98–99, 103–5, 107, 109, 115–18, 121–22, 132

B

Ball (neighbor of Ivy), 77–78, 83
Ball (teacher of Ivy), 97, 99–100
Baltimore, 1–2, 11, 22–23, 25–27, 30, 33, 36, 43, 85, 90, 161–67, 174
Barb (daughter of Betsy and Clarence), 15, 36
Barry (suitor of Ivy), 157–58, 161, 167, 175
Ben (adoptive father of Ivy), 7–9, 21–23, 27–31, 39–44, 46–47, 60–63, 66–69, 75–78, 82–84, 89–92, 123–24, 130–34, 141–43, 154–55, 161–64
Betsy (wife of Clarence), 15, 36–38, 40, 43, 45
Betty (friend of Ivy), 115, 140, 165

Bible school, 65, 67–70
Blackie (dog), 21, 84
Bob (uncle of Ivy), 9, 18, 22–23, 33, 45–48, 54–55, 61, 65–67, 71, 90–91, 98, 100, 102–3, 133, 143
brainwashing, 41–43, 61
Brownie (dog), 79, 81, 84
Brut (team manager), 121–22, 129
Bud (friend of Ivy), 136–37
Byrd (leader of the Junior Girls' Auxiliary), 94–95

C

Calloway (teacher of Ivy), 50
Churchill, Winston, 22
Church of God, 87
Clarence (uncle of Ivy), 15–16, 36–37, 55
Clay, Nancy, 120–21, 130

D

Dean (Sunday school teacher), 72, 85
Domino, Fats, 153
Donald (classmate of Ivy), 59, 73–74, 132
Donnelly (pastor's wife), 72–73

E

Ed (boyfriend of Ivy), 135–61,
    164–78
Eisenhower, Dwight D., 22, 118, 123
Eliz (mother of Jill), 103, 135
Emma (aunt of Ivy), 13–15, 20, 33

F

First Baptist Church, 94

G

Gladys (neighbor of Ivy), 75–76
Glen (son of Mrs. Ball), 78
God, vii, ix–x, 57, 93, 101–2, 119, 137
graduation, 126–29, 149, 176
Gray (neighbor of Ivy), 81, 87,
    119–21

H

Hitler, Adolf, 4–5, 8, 22, 45

J

Jake (cousin of Ivy), 139–40
James (schoolteacher), 58–59
Jan (ranch owner), 150–51
Jean (friend of Ivy), 136–37
Jean (Sunday school teacher), 72, 85
Jesus Christ, ix–xi, 57, 67, 70, 79, 93,
    101, 113–14, 118
"Jesus Loves Me," ix, 57, 65, 67, 70,
    79, 101, 118
Jill (friend of Ivy), 115, 125–26, 135,
    171
Jim (bandmate of Ivy), 104–5

Joanne (best friend of Ivy), 59, 88,
    94, 107, 115
John (adoptive brother of Ivy), 7,
    11–13, 16–17, 23–27, 30–32,
    35–38, 48, 55–56, 69–70,
    76–77, 87–88, 90–91, 112–13,
    115, 133
Johnson (church mate of Ivy), 57–
    58, 64, 72
Junior Girls' Auxiliary, 94

K

Karl (pastor), 114
Kee Street Methodist Church, ix,
    57, 93
Ken (husband of Emma), 14
Korea, 103, 118, 121, 123, 130
Korean conflict, 103, 108, 117–18,
    121–23, 129–30
Korean War, 103, 111, 116

L

Leo (brother of Emma), 14
Louise (classmate of Ivy), 108, 120

M

Maggie (friend of Ivy), 126–27,
    159–61, 168–69
Mama (mother of Mary), 12, 14–15,
    50, 81–83, 106–7, 133, 136,
    140, 143, 152
Marsha (cousin of Ivy), 1–2
Martha (real mother of Ivy), 1–3, 5,
    8, 11, 15, 23, 28, 31, 57, 110,
    161–64, 166–67
Mary (aunt and adoptive mother
    of Ivy), 10–13, 18–28, 32–43,
    45–46, 55–58, 60–63, 65–68,

78–79, 81–83, 86–93, 95–97,
100–101, 143–45, 149–52,
163–64
Mattie (ex-girlfriend of Ed), 168–70
missionaries, 94, 101–2
Morse, Samuel, 144

N

Nob School, 23, 27, 37, 88–89, 94,
103, 112, 127, 129, 132

O

Ohio, 114, 133–34, 139, 141, 143,
149–50, 154–55
Ooking (grandfather of Ivy), 1–6,
8–9, 11–12, 15–18, 20–23,
44, 46–48, 51–52, 54, 56–57,
64–65, 67–68, 79–80, 85–86,
130–33

P

Pam (mother of Ed), 135, 154
Pat (wife of Bob), 133, 143, 167
Pat (wife of Leo), 14
Patsy (friend of Ivy), ix, 51–52, 57,
82

R

rape, 43–44, 162
Ray (suitor of Ivy), 127–29, 150,
159–61, 166, 171, 175–76
Roosevelt, Franklin D., 22, 45, 152

S

Sally (friend of Ivy), 80, 96–98, 106,
115–17, 121, 129, 159, 171,
174–75
Seth (friend of Ivy), 125–26, 129
Sherry (daughter of Alfred and
Sue), 13, 52, 62
Shirley (friend of Ivy), 73–75
Shot (teacher of Ivy), 132, 145
Steve (adoptive brother of Ivy), 11–
12, 16, 23–27, 30–32, 48–50,
87–88, 90–91, 106–7, 109,
138–41, 144–46, 150–52,
162, 166–67, 173–74
Sue (aunt of Ivy), 13–14, 50–51
Sunday school, ix, 57, 93, 142, 174
Susie (adoptive sister of Ivy), 7–8,
10–13, 17–19, 26, 50–53, 57–
67, 69, 80–82, 85–88, 90–91,
93, 95–98, 140–43, 149–51,
162–67

T

Tabor (school teacher), 103, 108–9,
111
Temple, Shirley, 50, 59
Terri (schoolmate of Ivy), 94–95,
145, 149
Truman, Harry S., 45, 47, 103

W

whippings, 33, 60, 63, 75, 105, 114
World War II, 17, 22, 33, 36, 45, 50,
103, 119, 123, 130, 133, 150

Printed in the United States
By Bookmasters